A Pocketful
of
Herbs

Jekka
McVicar

A Pocketful
of
Herbs

Jekka
McVicar

BLOOMSBURY ABSOLUTE
LONDON · OXFORD · NEW YORK · NEW DELHI · SYDNEY

To Mac, Hannah and Alistair with love.

Contents

Introduction

Throughout our history, herbs have been the foundation of our medicine, a major component in the kitchen, and essential in the home. Quite simply, herbs are an indispensable part of our lives.

Personally, I don't think there is anything better than picking fresh herbs from the garden or just from the pots on the windowsill and adding them to a meal. This can transform pasta into a feast, a jacket potato into a tasty meal or a salad into a flavour explosion. Alternatively, you can put a fresh sprig of mint, rosemary or lemon verbena into a mug and add boiled water to make a delicious herbal infusion.

This book has evolved from my fascination with herbs and contains the knowledge I have gathered during the past 40 years of growing, exhibiting and using herbs. It contains details for over 400 herbs from all around the world and reflects the collection of culinary plants at my farm, Jekka's Herbetum.

I designed this book to be a complete reference that can fit into a bag or a backpack and can be used to jog the memory and help with identification; ideal for when you visit a garden or are on a walk and see a herb for which you cannot quite remember its family or what situation it prefers. For those who enjoy foraging wild herbs, it can reassure you as to what is actually edible.

Like the Herbetum, this book groups herbs into their families and common characteristics, such as mat forming, creeping or upright for thymes, making it simple to use. The book uses botanical names, which is common throughout the world, but I also include the colloquial UK name. I wish to provide you with a complete reference book and each herb is illustrated with a photograph and has a description of how and where the herb grows, as well as how it can be used. This includes the Royal Horticulture Society's hardiness level, the soil type and acidity and the amount of sun the herb prefers.

For whatever reason you use this book I hope it will become a good companion as you journey into the wonderful world of herbs.

Jekka McVicar
Bristol, 2019

botanical name

genus   *species*   *cultivar*

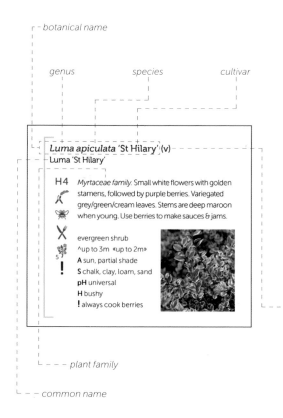

***Luma apiculata* 'St Hilary'** (v)
Luma 'St Hilary'

H 4   *Myrtaceae family.* Small white flowers with golden stamens, followed by purple berries. Variegated grey/green/cream leaves. Stems are deep maroon when young. Use berries to make sauces & jams.

evergreen shrub
^up to 3m «up to 2m»
A sun, partial shade
S chalk, clay, loam, sand
pH universal
H bushy
! always cook berries

plant family

common name

Plant Name

Botanical name includes the **genus** and, where appropriate, the **species** plus in some cases the **cultivar**. For example *Luma* is the genus, *apiculata* is the species and 'St Hilary' is the cultivar. The botanical name is known throughout the world.

Common name is the name by which the herb is commonly known, for example thyme, sage etc. But please be aware that common names are often colloquial and relevant to the area in which you find them.

Plant family is the group of plants which is more comprehensive than the genus. I find it really useful to find out from which family the plant comes, as this helps with identification, how to grow it, how to prune it and how to propagate it. I often recognise the family before I can remember the name. The largest family in my Herbetum is the Lamiaceae family, which consists mostly of shrubs and herbs that can be found all over the world. It includes plants such as mint, sage, thyme, basil, lavender, rosemary and also coleus and nettles to name just a few. You will find the family name identified for each of the herbs in this book.

- - - - - **(v)** denotes a variegated plant.

Luma apiculata 'St Hilary' (v)
Luma 'St Hilary'

H4 *Myrtaceae family.* Small white flowers with golden stamens, followed by purple berries. Variegated grey/green/cream leaves. Stems are deep maroon when young. Use berries to make sauces & jams.

X
5

evergreen shrub
^up to 3m «up to 2m»
A sun, partial shade
S chalk, clay, loam, sand
pH universal
H bushy
! always cook berries

Plant Type

Annual a plant that lives for just one season.

Biennial a plant that produces leaves in the first season and flowers in the second, then dies.

Climber/Vine a plant that cannot grow without the support of other plants or structures.

Deciduous a plant that drops its leaves in winter.

Dioecious a plant that has male and female flowers on different plants.

Evergreen a plant that has leaves all winter.

Herbaceous a plant that dies back into the ground in winter, becoming dormant, before reappearing in the spring.

Monocarpic a plant that dies once it flowers; it can live for a number of years before flowering.

Partial evergreen a plant that holds some leaves throughout the winter.

Perennial a plant that lives for a number of seasons, most flower annually once established.

Shrub a woody stemmed plant that usually freely branches from the base.

Sub-shrub a small, short, woody shrub, especially one that is woody only at the base.

Sub-tropical a plant that can only survive in a warm, damp climate that does not drop below 10°C at night.

Tree a woody plant that usually has a single stem.

Tropical a plant that can only survive in a warm, damp climate that does not drop below 15°C at night.

How to Use This Book

Luma apiculata 'St Hilary' (v)
Luma 'St Hilary'

H4 *Myrtaceae family.* Small white flowers with golden
 stamens, followed by purple berries. Variegated
grey/green/cream leaves. Stems are deep maroon
when young. Use berries to make sauces & jams.

evergreen shrub
^up to 3m «up to 2m»
5 **A** sun, partial shade
! **S** chalk, clay, loam, sand
pH universal
H bushy
! always cook berries

^Height «Spread»

This indicates the average height and spread that the plant will achieve in its life. It helps to know this when positioning plants in the garden.

Bear in mind, that height and spread vary in definition according to the following plant types:

Annual this is the spread to which it will grow, and the height when in flower during the year.

Biennial this is the spread in the first year and the height of the flower in the second year.

Herbaceous perennial and **perennial** this is the spread the plant will achieve after a number of years once mature and the height when in flower.

Shrub/evergreen tree this is the average spread and final height after a number of years of growth.

Aspect / Sunlight

Recommended planting position in the garden or where to place a pot, e.g. sun, partial shade etc.

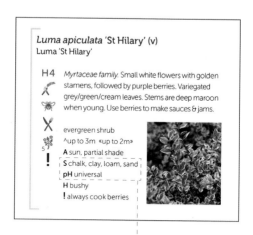

> ### *Luma apiculata* 'St Hilary' (v)
> Luma 'St Hilary'
>
> H4   *Myrtaceae family.* Small white flowers with golden stamens, followed by purple berries. Variegated grey/green/cream leaves. Stems are deep maroon when young. Use berries to make sauces & jams.
>
> evergreen shrub
> ^up to 3m «up to 2m»
> **A** sun, partial shade
> **S** chalk, clay, loam, sand
> **pH** universal
> **H** bushy
> **!** always cook berries

Soil Types and pH

The soil is the engine of your garden, so it is important to know its condition before you start planting. Good plant growth is dependent not only on how much you feed the soil but also on the structure of the soil. Soil can vary from acidic (pH 3.5) sphagnum moss peat to alkaline (pH 8.5) fine loam. Most herbs will tolerate a range of between 6.5 and 7.5 pH which is fairly neutral, and for quick reference in this book I have called this range 'universal pH'. There are always exceptions; for instance *Rumex scutatus*, sorrel, will tolerate acid soils.

The pH of the soil refers to its acidity or alkalinity. It is a vital factor in the plant's ability to obtain, via its roots system, all types of plant foods and essential chemicals. For example, an alkaline soil can produce stunted plants with yellowing leaves. This is because the minerals, especially iron, have become locked up in the soil. At a neutral pH of 7, most of the essential chemicals and plant foods become available to the plant, thus producing healthy plants.

The following 4 basic soil types are the most suitable for growing herbs:

Clay 6.5 pH This soil is composed of tiny particles that, when wet, stick together making the soil heavy and difficult for the roots to penetrate and in summer, when dry, sets rock hard. Even though it can be rich in plant nutrients, because of its characteristics it is improved by working in extra well rotted leaf mould or compost. This will improve the structure and allow young plants to become more easily established.

Chalk 8.5 pH This soil is light with lumps of flint or chalk, well-drained and often shallow. It has a high pH making it very alkaline. It is possible to increase the nutrient content by adding loads of compost but it is difficult to lower the pH. A large number of herbs will tolerate chalk. However, considering the characteristics of this soil, to give it depth and help it retain moisture it may be easier to grow the herbs in a raised bed.

Loam 5.5–8.5 pH This is often considered the ultimate garden soil in which most herbs will grow. There are various types of loam depending on the content of clay or sand. A sandy loam is the best soil for growing the largest range of herbs as it is rarely waterlogged in winter, is dry in summer and is naturally high in nutrients.

Sand 4.5 pH This soil feels rough and gritty when handled. It is very free draining, which means that the plant's nutrients are quickly washed away. A plus point to this soil is that it is quick to warm up in the spring so sowing and planting can be started earlier than in clay soils. To help it retain moisture it needs to be fed in winter with leaf mould to retain moisture and with well rotted manure for an extra source of nutrients.

Checking the pH of the soil

To test your soil buy a soil testing kit from any good garden centre or store. The majority of amateur soil testing kits are very simple and rely on colour rather than a numerical scale. Acid soils turn a solution yellow-orange, neutral turn it green and alkaline turn it a dark green.

Luma apiculata 'St Hilary' (v)
Luma 'St Hilary'

H4 *Myrtaceae family.* Small white flowers with golden
stamens, followed by purple berries. Variegated
grey/green/cream leaves. Stems are deep maroon
when young. Use berries to make sauces & jams.

X evergreen shrub
^up to 3m «up to 2m»
A sun, partial shade
S chalk, clay, loam, sand
pH universal
H bushy
! always cook berries

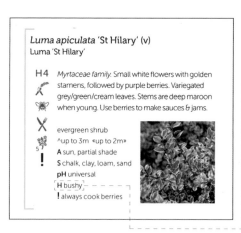

Habit

Plants grow in many shapes and forms:

Upright a plant that is straight and grows vertically.

Clump a plant that grows in a neat compact shape.

Bulb a plant that dies back into a bulb.

Mat forming a plant that grows low to the ground and makes a neat mat.

Creeping a plant that grows along the ground and produces roots at intervals.

Bushy a plant that, in the main, tends to be a shrub which makes a bush-like shape.

Arching a plant that grows upright first, after which the growth arches, ideal for growing over a wall or in a container.

Prostrate a plant that lies flat on the ground.

How to Use This Book

Luma apiculata 'St Hilary' (v)
Luma 'St Hilary'

H4

Myrtaceae family. Small white flowers with golden stamens, followed by purple berries. Variegated grey/green/cream leaves. Stems are deep maroon when young. Use berries to make sauces & jams.

evergreen shrub
^up to 3m ‹up to 2m›
A sun, partial shade
S chalk, clay, loam, sand
pH universal
H bushy
! always cook berries

Symbols

See the cover flaps for a breakdown of all the symbols that appear within these pages.

Hardiness

All ratings refer to UK growing conditions and are based on the Royal Horticultural Society hardiness rating. The minimum temperature range, in degrees centigrade, are shown in the brackets below.

H1a (15°C minimum)
Under glass all year.

H1b (10°C to 15°C)
Can be grown outside in summer.

H1c (5°C to 10°C)
Can be grown outside in summer.

H2 (1°C to 5°C)
Tolerant of low temperatures but will not survive being frozen.

H3 (-5°C to 1°C)
Hardy in coastal and relatively mild, sheltered parts of the UK.

H4 (-10°C to -5°C)
Hardy through most of the UK.

H5 (-15°C to -10°C)
Hardy in most places throughout the UK, even in severe winters.

H6 (-20°C to -15°C)
Hardy in all of the UK and northern Europe.

H7 (-20°C and below)
Hardy in the severest European continental climates.

Herbs by Botanical name

Achillea ageratum
English Mace

H4 *Asteracea family.* Clusters of small creamy daisy-flowers. Aromatic, mid-green, pinnately divided, toothed leaves. Mild-flavoured leaves used in soups, stews, vegetable, chicken & egg dishes.

herbaceous perennial
^30–45cm «60cm»
A full sun
S clay, sand
pH universal
H upright

Achillea millefolium
Yarrow, Woundwort, Milfoil

H6 *Asteracea family.* Small white to pale pink flowers grouped in flat clusters. Green, aromatic, feathery foliage. Use young leaves in salads or with vegetables.

herbaceous perennial
^30–90cm «60cm»
A full sun
S clay, sand
pH universal
H mat forming, creeping
! can irritate skin; do not take if pregnant

Acinos alpinus
Alpine Basil, Basil Thyme

H4 *Lamiaceae family.* Small-lipped pink/mauve flowers. Highly aromatic small grey/green leaves. Flowers & leaves are edible. Leaves are good with meat, vegetable, rice & pasta dishes.

herbaceous perennial
^20cm «70cm»
A full sun
S light loam, sand, free draining
pH universal
H mat forming, creeping

Agastache foeniculum (Pursh) Kuntze
Anise Hyssop

H3 *Lamiaceae family.* Long purple flower spikes.
Aniseed-scented, oval, toothed, mid-green
leaves. Flowers used in sweet & savoury salads.
Leaves used in salads & for making tisanes.

herbaceous perennial
^70cm «30cm»
A full sun, partial shade
S light loam, sand,
   free draining
pH universal
H upright

Agastache rugosa
Korean Mint, Huo Xiang

H3 *Lamiaceae family.* Lovely mauve/purple tubular
flower spikes. Mint-scented, oval, toothed, mid-
green leaves. Flowers & leaves are edible, use in
stir fry dishes & salads.

herbaceous perennial
^up to 1m «30cm»
A full sun, partial shade
S light loam, sand,
   free draining
pH universal
H upright

Agastache rugosa 'Golden Jubilee'
Golden Agastache

H3 *Lamiaceae family.* Purple tubular flower spikes.
Aniseed-scented, oval, toothed, golden leaves
that are prone to sun scorch. Use flowers in
sweet & savoury salads, & leaves in salads.

herbaceous perennial
^50cm «20cm»
A partial shade
S light loam, sand,
   free draining
pH universal
H upright

Allium cepa Proliferum Group
Tree Onion, Catawissa Onion

H5 *Alliaceae family.* Small greenish white flowers in 2nd year, followed by small bulbs that form at the top of the stem. Hollow cylindrical mid-green leaves. Whole plant is edible.

perennial
^up to 1.5m «20cm»
A sun
S loam, fertile sand, free draining
pH universal
H bulb

Allium fistulosum
Welsh Onion, Japanese Leek

H5 *Alliaceae family.* Large creamy white globe-shaped flowers in the 2nd year. Hollow cylindrical mid-green leaves. Whole plant is edible. Use with egg, cheese & stir fry dishes.

perennial
^50cm «50cm»
A sun
S loam, fertile sand, free draining
pH universal
H clump

Allium fistulosum 'Red Welsh'
Red Welsh Onion

H5 *Alliaceae family.* Large creamy white globe-shaped flowers in the 2nd year. Hollow cylindrical mid-green leaves with a red tinge at the base. Whole plant is edible, use in salads.

perennial
^50cm «50cm»
A sun
S loam, fertile sand, free draining
pH universal
H bulb

Allium nutans
Siberian Chives, Blue Chives

H6 *Alliaceae family.* Blue/mauve star-shaped flowers. Flat, solid, narrow, lance-shaped green leaves, mild onion/garlic flavour. Use leaves & flowers in salads, vegetable & dairy dishes.

perennial
^40cm «15cm»
A sun
S loam, fertile sand,
   free draining
pH universal
H clump

Allium sativum
Garlic

H5 *Alliaceae family.* White or pink flowers. Lance-shaped, green leaves. Bulb is made of several cloves, which can vary in colour from white to pink. Whole plant is edible, use in savoury dishes.

perennial
^40–60cm «10cm»
A sun
S light loam, sand,
   free draining
pH universal
H bulb

Allium schoenoprasum
Chives

H5 *Alliaceae family.* Purple globe-shaped flowers. Narrow cylindrical, mid-green leaves. Both the leaves & flowers are edible, with a mild onion flavour. Add to salads, egg & cheese dishes.

herbaceous perennial
^30cm «30cm»
A sun
S loam, fertile sand,
   free draining
pH universal
H clump

Allium schoenoprasum 'Cha Cha'
Cha Cha Chives

H5   *Alliaceae family.* Rather than actual flowers, mini cylindrical green leaves grow in the flower heads. Narrow cylindrical, mid-green leaves. Use mini chives & leaves in salads.

 herbaceous perennial
^45cm «30cm»
A sun
S loam, fertile sand,
   free draining
pH universal
H clump

Allium schoenoprasum 'Forescate'
Pink Chives

H5   *Alliaceae family.* Pink globe-shaped flowers. Narrow cylindrical, mid-green leaves. Both the leaves & flowers have a mild onion flavour. Add to salads, egg & cheese dishes.

 herbaceous perennial
^45cm «30cm»
A sun
S loam, fertile sand,
   free draining
pH universal
H clump

Allium tuberosum
Garlic Chives, Chinese Chives

H5   *Alliaceae family.* White star-shaped flowers. Flat, solid, narrow, lance-shaped, green, mild garlic-flavoured leaves. Use leaves & flowers in salads.

 perennial
^60cm «30cm»
A sun
S light loam, sand,
   free draining
pH universal
H clump

Allium ursinum
Ramsons, Wild Garlic, Wood Garlic

H6 *Alliaceae family.* White star-shaped flowers. Broad lance-shaped, green, garlic-flavoured leaves. Flowers & leaves are edible. Eat leaves before flowering, they make a very good pesto.

herbaceous perennial
^45cm «indefinite»
A partial shade
S chalk, loam, sand,
   free draining
pH universal
H clump

Allium vineale
Wild Onion, Crow Garlic

H6 *Alliaceae family.* Creamy/beige flowers. Thin, chive-like, mid-green leaves. Use in salads, with roast potatoes & with egg dishes. Invasive.

herbaceous perennial
^60cm «indefinite»
A sun
S clay, loam, sand
pH universal
H upright
! poisonous to dogs

Aloe vera
Aloe, Barbados Aloe, Bitter Aloes

H1c *Asphodelacea family.* Yellow or orange bell-shaped flowers appear on mature plants. Grey/green fleshy spear-shaped leaves with spiny edges. Apply gel from the leaf d to minor burns.

evergreen perennial
^60cm «60cm»
A full sun
S light loam, sand
pH universal
H mat forming
! do not self-medicate

Aloysia citrodora
Lemon Verbena

H3 *Verbenaceae family.* Delicate small white flowers. Highly fragrant lemon-scented, narrow oval, rough textured, mid-green leaves. Use leaves in drinks, jams, jellies, ice cream & cakes.

deciduous shrub
^up to 3m «up to 2.5m»
A full sun
S light loam,
 free draining
pH universal
H bushy

Aloysia gratissima
White Brush

H3 *Verbenaceae family.* Delicate small, slightly vanilla-scented, white or violet-tinged flowers. Small, lance-shaped, spearmint-scented, grey/green leaves. Use in drinks, sorbets & with fruit.

deciduous shrub
^up to 3m «up to 2m»
A full sun
S light loam,
 free draining
pH universal
H arching, bushy

Althaea officinalis
Marsh-mallow

H6 *Malvaceae family.* Pink/white flowers. Velvety, round to ovate, grey/green leaves. Roots are edible, traditionally used to thicken a broth.

herbaceous perennial
^up to 1.5m «60cm»
A partial shade
S clay, loam,
 free draining
pH universal
H clump

Amaranthus tricolor 'Red Army'
Amaranth

H2 *Amaranthaceae family.* Long-lasting small
 red flowers, followed by seeds which are edible
 when cooked. Ovate, textured, red leaves. Use
young leaves in salads & seeds in flat breads.

annual
^up to 1.5m «30cm»
A full sun
S clay, loam, sand,
  free draining
pH neutral–alkaline
H upright

Amomyrtus luma
Amomyrtus

H4 *Myrtaceae family.* White flowers with yellow
stamens, followed by black/blue berries. Small
pointed, green/brown, aromatic leaves. Spring
growth is copper-coloured. Use berries for jams.

evergreen tree
^up to 25m «up to 4m
A sun
S damp loam
pH acid–neutral
H tree
! always cook berries

Anethum graveolens
Dill

H4 *Apiaceae family.* Umbels of small yellow/
green flowers followed by aromatic seeds.
Fine, feathery, aromatic, mid-green leaves. Use
leaves, flowers & seeds in pickles & salads.

annual
^up to 1.5m «20cm»
A sun, partial shade
S light loam, sand,
  free draining
pH universal
H upright

Angelica archangelica
Angelica

H5 *Apiaceae family.* Round umbels of white/green, sweetly scented flowers in 2nd year. Large, bright green, deeply divided leaves. Flowers & leaves are edible, as are the stems when cooked.

monocarpic

 ^up to 2.5m «up to 1m»

A sun, partial shade

S damp loam

pH universal

H upright

! do not self-medicate; can cause dermatitis

Anthriscus cerefolium
Chervil

H4 *Apiaceae family.* Tiny white flowers in 2nd year. Light green, anise-flavoured leaves which often develop a purple tinge in drought or early autumn. One of the original 'Fines Herbes'.

biennial

^up to 60cm «25cm»

A sun, partial shade

S loam, fertile sand, free draining

pH universal

H upright

Apium graveolens
Celery Leaf, Wild Celery

H5 *Apiaceae family.* Clusters of green white flowers in 2nd year followed by aromatic seeds. Mid-green cut leaves have a strong celery flavour. Use young leaves & seeds in soups & salads.

biennial

^30cm–1m «30cm»

A sun, partial shade

S loam, fertile sand, free draining

pH universal

H upright

! can cause dermatitis

Aralia racemosa
American Spikenard

H7 *Araliaceae family.* Umbels of small greenish/
white flowers followed by tiny edible black/blue
berries. Large pinnate mid-green leaves which
have good autumn colour. Use berries in jams.

herbaceous perennial
^up to 1.5m «up to 1.5m»
A sun, partial shade
S fertile loam
pH universal
H bushy

Armoracia rusticana
Horseradish

H6 *Brassicaceae family.* Tiny white flowers. Mid-
green, crinkled textured leaves. Harvest roots in
autumn. Great with apples, avocados, mackerel
& beef. Invasive.

perennial
^90cm «indefinite»
A sun, partial shade
S clay, loam
pH acid–neutral
H clump
! do not self-medicate

Armoracia rusticana 'Variegata' (v)
Variegated Horseradish

H6 *Brassicaceae family.* Tiny white flowers.
Mid-green & white variegated leaves in spring.
Harvest roots in autumn. Great with apples,
avocados, mackerel & beef. Invasive.

perennial
^75cm «indefinite»
A sun, partial shade
S clay, loam
pH acid–neutral
H clump
! do not self-medicate

Artemisia abrotanum
Southernwood, Lads Love

H5 *Asteraceae family.* Rarely flowers in UK; if it does the flowers are tiny & light green in colour. Grey/green, finely divided, aromatic, feathery foliage. Excellent moth repellent.

deciduous shrub
^1m «1m»
A full sun
S light loam,
   free draining
pH universal
H bushy
! do not use if pregnant

Artemisia absinthium
Wormwood

H5 *Asteraceae family.* Tiny yellow flowers. Silver/green, divided, aromatic foliage. Leaves & flowers are very bitter. Good with cheese. Used in many drinks such as Absinthe & Vermouth.

deciduous perennial
^1m «1m»
A full sun
S light loam,
   free draining
pH universal
H bushy
! do not self-medicate

Artemisia alba
Camphor Scented Southernwood

H5 *Asteraceae family.* Small light green flowers. Aromatic, finely divided, feathery, grey/green foliage. The foliage has a lovely camphor scent, good for use as a moth repellent.

deciduous shrub
^1m «1m»
A full sun
S light loam, free draining
pH universal
H bushy
! do not use if pregnant

Artemisia annua
Sweet Wormwood, Sweet Annie

H2   *Asteraceae family.* Tiny yellow flowers clustered in loose panicles. Aromatic, finely cut, bright green leaves. Endorsed by WHO (World Health Organisation) for the treatment of malaria.

annual
^up to 3m «up to 1.5m»
A full sun
S light loam,
 free draining
pH universal
H upright
! do not use if pregnant

Artemisia dracunculus
French Tarragon

H4   *Asteraceae family.* Rarely flowers in the UK; if it does the flowers are pale green in colour. Long, narrow, smooth, aromatic, green leaves with anise flavour. Use with fish, chicken & soups.

herbaceous perennial
^90cm «45cm»
A full sun
S light loam,
 free draining
pH universal
H upright

Atriplex hortensis var. rubra
Red Orach

H2   *Chenopodiaceae family.* Small racemes of tiny red flowers which are followed by round disc seeds. Dark red leaves. Use young leaves in salads; steam mature leaves; use seeds in bread.

annual
^up to 1m «30cm»
A sun, partial shade
S fertile, light loam
pH universal
H upright

Backhousia citriodora
Lemon Myrtle

H2 *Myrtaceae family.* Beautiful clusters of cream flowers. Lemon-scented & flavoured, lance-shaped, mid-green leaves. Use leaves to flavour oils & vinegars. Traditional Australian bush food.

sub-tropical evergreen
  tree
^up to 20m «up to 10m»
A sun
S light loam,
  free draining
pH acid–neutral
H bushy

Bergera koenigii
Curry Tree, Curry Leaf

H1c *Rutaceae family.* Clusters of fragrant star-shaped white flowers, followed by black oval berries. Thin, ovate, shiny, dark green, very aromatic leaves. Use leaves in curries & to flavour rice.

evergreen shrub
^up to 6m «up to 5m»
A full sun
S loam, free draining
pH universal
H bushy
! do not ingest seeds

Beta vulgaris 'Bulls Blood'
Bulls Blood Beetroot

H5 *Amaranthaceae family.* Clusters of small green flowers in 2nd year. Red leaves. Use young leaves in salads. Pull the roots to eat as beetroot when large enough. Slow release sugar.

biennial
^30cm «15cm»
A sun
S fertile light loam
pH neutral–alkaline
H clump

Beta vulgaris 'Ruby Chard'
Rhubarb Chard

H5 *Amaranthaceae family.* Clusters of small
green flowers in 2nd year. Red ribbed leaves.
Young leaves can be eaten raw or steamed &
served as a vegetable.

biennial
^45cm «25cm»
A sun
S fertile light loam
pH neutral–alkaline
H clump

Borago officinalis
Borage

H4 *Boraginaceae family.* Blue star-shaped flowers.
Mid-green, oval, bristly, slightly succulent leaves.
Use flowers in drinks & salads. Use young leaves
in salads & soups. Seeds are high in GLA.

annual
^60cm «60cm»
A full sun
S chalk, loam, sand,
free draining
pH universal
H upright
! can cause dermatitis

Borago officinalis 'Alba'
White Borage

H4 *Boraginaceae family.* Attractive star-shaped white
flowers. Mid-green, oval, bristly, slightly succulent
leaves. Use flowers in drinks & salads. Use young
leaves in salads. Seeds are high in GLA.

annual
^45cm «45cm»
A full sun
S chalk, loam, sand,
free draining
pH universal
H upright
! can cause dermatitis

Borago pygmaea
Prostrate Borage, Corsican Borage

H4   *Boraginaceae family.* Lovely pale blue small
    star-shaped flowers. Rough, bristly, oval, green
leaves. Good ground cover. Flowers can be
    used in drinks & salads.

    evergreen perennial
^30cm «45cm»
A full sun
    S chalk, loam, sand,
     free draining
    pH universal
H prostrate
! can cause dermatitis

Brassica juncea 'Golden Streaks'
Golden Mustard

H3   *Brassicaceae family.* Yellow flowers followed
by long seed pods with brown seeds. Attractive
golden green, narrow indented leaves. Leaves &
flowers are edible. Grind seeds to make mustard.

    annual
^15cm «15cm»
A sun, partial shade
S fertile loam
pH acid–neutral
!   **H** clump
! seeds can cause
     allergic reaction

Brassica juncea 'Red Frills'
Red Frills Mustard

H3   *Brassicaceae family.* Yellow flowers followed
by long seed pods with brown seeds. Attractive
dark red, narrow indented leaves. Leaves &
    flowers are edible. Grind seeds to make mustard.

annual
    ^15cm «15cm»
A sun, partial shade
    S fertile loam
pH acid–neutral
!   **H** clump
! seeds can cause
     allergic reaction

Bulbine frutescens
African Bulbine, Burn Jelly Plant

H3   *Asphodelacea family.* Clusters of star-shaped yellow & orange flowers appear throughout the summer. Clumps of succulent, linear fleshy, green leaves. Sap can be applied to minor burns.

   evergreen perennial
^60cm–1m «1–1.5m»
A full sun
S light loam, sand, free draining
pH neutral–alkaline
H clump
! do not use if pregnant

Calamintha grandiflora
Large Flowered Calamint

H5   *Lamiaceae family.* Dense whorls of lilac/pink flowers. Lightly mint-scented, oval, green, toothed leaves. Young leaves are good in marinades & for use in tisanes.

herbaceous perennial
^45cm «30cm»
A full sun
S light loam, sand, free draining
pH neutral–alkaline
H clump

Calamintha menthifolia
Calamint, Mountain Balm

H5   *Lamiaceae family.* Small pale pink flowers. Mint-scented oval, toothed leaves. Both the leaves & flowers are edible, use with meat & vegetable dishes. Good for tisanes.

   herbaceous perennial
^60cm «45cm»
A full sun
S light loam, sand, free draining
pH neutral–alkaline
H clump

Calamintha nepeta
Lesser Calamint

H5 *Lamiaceae family.* Small purple/white flowers. Small grey/green oval leaves covered in fine hairs. Whole plants is aromatic. Flowers & leaves are edible. Leaves are great with mushrooms.

herbaceous perennial
^30cm «30cm»
A full sun
S light loam, sand, free draining
pH neutral–alkaline
H clump

Calendula officinalis
Pot Marigold

H3 *Asteraceae family.* Large daisy-like orange/yellow single flowers throughout the season until the first frosts. Lance-shaped, slightly hairy, green leaves. Use flower petals in salads.

annual
^up to 60cm «30cm»
A full sun, partial shade
S chalk, loam, sand, free draining
pH universal
H upright

Calendula officinalis Fiesta Gitana Group
Marigold Fiesta Gitana

H3 *Asteraceae family.* Large daisy-like orange/yellow double flowers throughout the season until the first frosts. Lance-shaped, slightly hairy, green leaves. Use flower petals in salads.

annual
^up to 35cm «up to 35cm»
A full sun, partial shade
S chalk, loam, sand, free draining
pH universal
H upright

Capparis spinosa
Caper

H3

Capparaceae family. Edible green buds followed by single white flowers with purple stamens. Oval mid-green tough/succulent leaves. Flower buds & seed pods can be pickled.

evergreen shrub
^up to 1.5m «up to 1.5m»
A full sun
S loam, sand,
    free draining
pH neutral–alkaline
H bushy, prostrate
! sharp spikes

Carum carvi
Caraway

H5

Apiaceae family. Tiny clusters of creamy white flowers in 2nd year. Feathery bright green leaves. Seeds used in cooking & baking. Young leaves used in salads.

biennial
^20–60cm «25cm»
A full sun
S loam, sand,
    free draining
pH acid–neutral
H upright

Cedronella canariensis
Balm of Gilead

H3

Lamiaceae family. Attractive pink/mauve 2-lipped flowers. Aromatic, camphor-scented, 3-lobed & tooth-edged, green leaves. An infusion of leaves is good for clearing the head.

partial evergreen shrub
^1m «60cm»
A sun, partial shade
S loam, sand,
    free draining
pH slightly alkaline
H upright

Centaurea cyanus
Cornflower

H3   *Asteraceae family.* Lovely bright blue flowers. Lance-shaped, grey/green leaves. Flower petals are edible & can be used to great effect scattered over salads, rice or in summer drinks.

annual
^up to 75cm «15cm»
A full sun
S loam, sand, free draining
pH neutral–alkaline
H upright

Centella asiatica
Gotu Kola, Indian Pennywort, Tiger Grass

H3   *Apiaceae family.* Tiny magenta flowers. Bright green, kidney-shaped leaves. Young leaves are eaten in eastern dishes & used as a vegetable in Sri Lanka & India. Traditional medicinal herb.

partial evergreen
^8cm «indefinite»
A partial shade
S damp loam
pH acid–neutral
H mat forming, creeping
! beware excessive use

Centranthus ruber
Red Valerian

H5   *Caprifoliaceae family.* Clusters of small trumpet-shaped pink/red flowers. Fleshy pale green, lance-shaped, pointed leaves. Bitter young leaves are eaten in Southern Europe in salads.

semi-evergreen perennial
^75cm «40cm»
A full sun
S chalk, loam, sand, free draining
pH neutral–alkaline
H upright
! do not self-medicate

Chamaemelum nobile
Chamomile, Roman Chamomile

H5 *Asteraceae family.* White petals with a yellow centre in summer. Sweet smelling, finely divided green leaves. Use flowers to make chamomile tea. An infusion can lighten fair hair.

evergreen perennial
^10–30cm «45cm»
A full sun
S chalk, loam, sand, free draining
pH universal
H upright
! do not self-medicate

Chamaemelum nobile 'Flore Pleno'
Double Flowered Chamomile

H5 *Asteraceae family.* Double white, daisy-like flowers. Dense aromatic finely divided green leaves. Good for lawns. Flowers can be used in infusions.

evergreen perennial
^8cm «30cm»
A full sun
S chalk, loam, sand, free draining
pH universal
H mat forming

Chamaemelum nobile 'Treneague'
Lawn Chamomile

H5 *Asteraceae family.* Non-flowering. Dense aromatic finely divided green leaves. Famous for making a non-mowing lawn or for making chamomile cushions.

evergreen perennial
^6cm «30cm»
A full sun
S chalk, loam, sand, free draining
pH universal
H mat forming

Chenopodium bonus-henricus
Good King Henry

H5 *Chenopodiaceae family.* Tiny greenish/yellow flowers. Mid-green large goose foot-shaped leaves. Steam flower spikes, use leaves in casseroles, stuffings & soups.

herbaceous perennial
^60cm «45cm»
A sun, partial shade
S fertile loam
pH universal
H clump

Chenopodium giganteum
Tree Spinach, Giant Goosefoot

H5 *Chenopodiaceae family.* Tiny green/yellow flowers. Mid-green, arrow-shaped leaves with serrated edges. New young growth is a magenta colour. Use young leaves in salads.

annual
^up to 2m «45cm»
A sun, partial shade
S fertile loam
pH universal
H upright

Cichorium intybus
Chicory, Succory

H5 *Asteraceae family.* Clear blue flowers in the 2nd year. Oval mid-green coarsely toothed leaves, with tiny hairs on the underside. Use young leaves & flowers in salads & the root for coffee.

herbaceous perennial
^up to 1m «30cm»
A full sun
S fertile light loam
pH acid–neutral
H upright
! do not use excessively

Claytonia perfoliata
Winter Purslane, Miner's Lettuce

H4 *Portulacaceae family.* Small white flowers
surrounded by large succulent green bracts.
Green, spear-shaped leaves. Whole plant is
edible, good as a winter crop. High in vitamins.

annual
^30cm «15cm»
A partial shade
S light loam, sand, free
draining
pH universal
H clump

Clinopodium vulgare
Wild Basil

H5 *Lamiaceae family.* Small pink/purple tubular
flowers. Small, hairy, lance-shaped, mid-green
leaves with serrated edges. Flowers & young
leaves are edible, use to flavour salads & tisanes.

herbaceous perennial
^up to 60cm «45cm»
A sun, partial shade
S light loam, sand, free
draining
pH universal
H clump

Coriandrum sativum
Coriander

H3 *Apiaceae family.* White flowers are followed by
round seeds. The first & lower mid-green leaves
are broad & scalloped with the best flavour.
Upper leaves are finely cut. Whole plant is edible.

annual
^up to 60cm «20cm»
A full sun, partial shade
S light loam
pH neutral–alkaline
H upright

Crambe maritima
Sea Kale

H4 *Brassicaceae family.* Honey-scented white
flowers. Fleshy grey/green leaves with crinkled
edges. Blanch leaves in autumn for eating in
spring. Leaves are rich in vitamin C & magnesium.

herbaceous perennial
^75cm «60cm»
A full sun, partial shade
S light loam, sand,
   free draining
pH neutral–alkaline
H upright

Crithmum maritimum
Rock Samphire, Sea Fennel

H4 *Apiaceae family.* Umbels of tiny yellow/green
flowers. The succulent sea green leaves are
oblong & high in vitamin C, with a strong salty
flavour. Great pickled or made into chutney.

herbaceous perennial
^30cm «30cm»
A full sun, partial shade
S light loam, sand,
   free draining
pH neutral–alkaline
H upright

Cryptotaenia japonica
Japanese Parsley, Mitsuba

H5 *Apiaceae family.* Small white flowers. Mid-green
leaves with serrated edges. Flowers, stems,
leaves & roots are edible. Young leaves can be
eaten raw, stems are best steamed.

herbaceous perennial
^30cm «30cm»
A partial shade, shade
S fertile light loam
pH universal
H upright

Curcuma longa
Turmeric

H1c  *Zingiberaceae family.* Yellow/white flowers with a pink tinge on the tips of the petals. Long, mid-green oval, aromatic leaves. Spreading rhizome root. Use roots in curries & eastern food.

tropical/subtropical
 herbaceous perennial
^up to 1m «indefinite»
A partial shade
S fertile light loam
pH acid–neutral
H upright
! do not ingest sap

Cymbopogon flexuosus
East Indian Lemongrass

H2 *Poaceae family.* Grass-like magenta flowers. Flowers only in the tropics or under protection. Lemon-scented, linear, grey/green leaves. Stems & leaves are edible & used for making tisanes.

evergreen perennial
^up to 1.5m «1m»
A full sun
S light loam, sand,
 free draining
pH acid
H upright
! do not ingest oil

Cynara cardunculus
Cardoon

H5 *Asteraceae family.* Large thistle-like blue/violet flowers in summer, large silver/grey serrated leaves. Blanch leaves in winter to produce edible leaf ribs. Use as a vegetable or in soups.

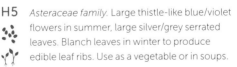
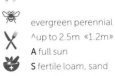

evergreen perennial
^up to 2.5m «1.2m»
A full sun
S fertile loam, sand
pH acid–neutral
H upright

D

Dianthus 'Mrs Sinkins'
Clove Pink Mrs Sinkins

H5 *Caryophyllaceae family.* Very fragrant, clove-scented, double white flowers. Narrow grey/green leaves. Flower petals can be eaten in salads & used to flavour vinegars.

evergreen perennial
^30cm «45cm»
A full sun
S chalk, loam, sand, free draining
pH neutral–alkaline
H clump

Dianthus 'Spring Star'
Clove Pink Spring Star

H5 *Caryophyllaceae family.* Pretty, clove-scented, pink flowers with a dark magenta centre. Narrow blue/grey leaves. Flower petals can be eaten in salads & used to flavour vinegars.

evergreen perennial
^20cm «20cm»
A full sun
S chalk, loam, sand, free draining
pH neutral–alkaline
H clump

Dianthus 'Whatfield Cancan'
Clove Pink Whatfield Cancan

H5 *Caryophyllaceae family.* Pretty, clove-scented, pink frilled double flowers. Narrow blue/green leaves. Flower petals can be eaten in salads & used to flavour vinegars.

evergreen perennial
^20cm «30cm»
A full sun
S chalk, loam, sand, free draining
pH neutral–alkaline
H clump

Digitalis purpurea
Foxglove, Fairy Gloves

H6 *Scrophulariaceae family.* Tubular purple or white flowers, with purple spots in the throat, in the 2nd year. Large textured, lance-shaped green leaves. Medicinal, used to regulate the heart.

biennial
^up to 1.8m «60cm»
A sun, partial shade
S loam, free draining
pH universal
H upright
! whole plant is poisonous

Diplotaxis muralis
Wild Rocket

H4 *Brassicaceae family.* Small yellow 4-petalled flowers. Green, deeply divided, aromatic leaves. The leaves are high in sulphur, good for healthy skin. Delicious in salads & with egg dishes.

perennial, often grown
  as annual
^30cm «15cm»
A sun, partial shade
S light loam
pH universal
H clump

Echinacea angustifolia
Black Sampson, Narrow Leaved Echinacea

H5 *Asteraceae family.* Flowers are single with long purple or, rarely, white petals, with a spiky central cone. Mid-green linear leaves. Root is used medicinally. Endangered from over-collection.

herbaceous perennial
^up to 60cm «30cm»
A full sun
S fertile light loam
pH universal
H upright
! can cause
  allergic reaction

Echinacea purpurea
Echinacea, Purple Coneflower

H5 · *Asteraceae family.* Large daisy-like purple/pink flowers with golden brown spiky cone that gets more pointed as it matures. Oval, mid-green, deeply veined leaves. Root used medicinally.

herbaceous perennial
^up to 1.2m «45cm»
A full sun
S fertile, light loam
pH universal
H upright
! can cause allergic reaction

Echium vulgare
Viper's Bugloss

H5 · *Boraginaceae family.* Very attractive bright blue/pink flowers in 2nd year. Renowned for self seeding. Mid-green, lance-shaped, bristly leaves that can cause skin irritation. Flowers are edible.

biennial
^50cm «40cm»
A full sun
S light loam, free draining
pH universal
H upright
! can cause dermatitis

Elettaria cardamomum
Cardamom

H2 · *Zingiberaceae family.* Orchid-like white flowers with a striped purple/pink lower lip, followed by aromatic seeds. Smooth, lance-shaped aromatic dark green leaves. Edible seeds; use leaves as a flavouring.

tropical, sub-tropical evergreen perennial
^up to 3m «indefinite»
A sun, partial shade
S loam
pH acid–neutral
H upright, creeping

E

Elsholtzia stauntonii
Mint Shrub, Mint Bush

H5 *Lamiaceae family.* Spikes of lilac flowers.
Lance-shaped mid-green leaves that turn red in
autumn. Medicinal Chinese plant. Excellent for
attracting butterflies & other pollinating insects.

deciduous shrub
^up to 1.2m «up to
1.2m»
A full sun
S fertile light loam
pH neutral
H bushy

Eriocephalus africanus
South African Wild Rosemary

H3 *Asteraceae family.* Clusters of white daisy-
like flowers with deep maroon centres. Grey,
aromatic, soft, hairy, thin leaves grow in tufts
along the branch. Use with meat & vegetables.

evergreen shrub
^up to 2m «1.5m»
A full sun
S light loam, sand,
free draining
pH light acid–neutral
H bushy
! do not use if pregnant

Eruca vesicaria subsp. *sativa*
Salad Rocket, Arugula

H3 *Brassicaceae family.* Flowers start yellow then
fade to cream with purple veins. Oval, lance-
shaped leaves with a nutty spicy flavour. Leaves
& flowers are edible; use in salads or for pesto.

annual
^up to 90cm «15cm»
A sun, partial shade
S light loam
pH neutral
H upright

49

Ferula assa-foetida
Assa-foetida, Devil's Dung, Hing

H4 *Apiaceae family.* Flowers in the 4th year with flat umbels of tiny yellow flowers. Flowering spikes can reach 4m. Large, finely divided, green, garlic-scented leaves. Use dried roots to flavour food.

herbaceous perennial
^up to 4m «1.5m»
A full sun
S light loam, free draining
pH universal
H upright
! not for children/babies

Ferula communis
Giant Fennel

H3 *Apiaceae family.* Striking round umbels of tiny yellow flowers. Large feathery dark green leaves which die back in summer reappearing in autumn. Traditional medicinal herb.

herbaceous perennial
^up to 4m «1.5m»
A full sun
S light loam, free draining
pH universal
H upright
! not for children/babies

Filipendula ulmaria
Meadowsweet

H6 *Rosaceae family.* Clusters of frothy, almond-scented, creamy white flowers. Aromatic, pinnate, serrated, deeply veined mid-green leaves. Flowers used to flavour drinks & vinegars.

herbaceous perennial
^up to 1.2m «60cm»
A sun, partial shade
S clay, loam
pH neutral–alkaline
H upright
! do not self-medicate

Foeniculum vulgare
Fennel

H5 *Apiaceae family.* Large flat umbels of small
yellow flowers, followed by aromatic seeds.
Soft green feathery foliage. Flower, seed & leaf
are edible. Use with fish, pork & all salads.

herbaceous perennial
^up to 2.1m «45cm»
A full sun
S light loam
pH neutral
H upright
! do not self-medicate

Foeniculum vulgare 'Purpureum'
Bronze Fennel

H4 *Apiaceae family.* Large flat umbels of small
yellow flowers, followed by aromatic seeds.
Striking bronze feathery foliage. Flower, seed &
leaf are edible. Use with fish, pork & all salads.

herbaceous perennial
^up to 2.1m «45cm»
A full sun
S light loam
pH neutral
H upright
! do not self-medicate

Fragaria vesca
Wild Strawberry

H6 *Rosaceae family.* Small white flowers followed
by small, edible, sweet, red fruit. Trifoliate, mid-
green, toothed leaves. Very young leaves used
in salads; fruit used in salads, puddings & drinks.

perennial
^30cm «indefinite»
A sun, partial shade
S clay, loam, sand
pH universal
H clump, creeping
! can cause allergic
reaction

Fragaria vesca 'White Delight'
White Fruiting Strawberry

H6

Rosaceae family. Small white flowers followed by small white, sweet, edible fruit. Trifoliate, mid-green, toothed leaves. Use young leaves in salads; use fruit in salads, puddings & drinks.

perennial
^30cm «indefinite»
A sun, partial shade
S clay, loam, sand
pH universal
H clump, creeping
! can cause allergic
reaction

Fuchsia arborescens
Tree Fuchsia

H1c *Onagraceae family.* Panicles of dark pink buds that open to small fragrant pink/purple flowers followed by round blue/black fruit. Glossy, mid to dark green, elliptic leaves. Use fruit for jelly.

evergreen shrub
^up to 2m «up to 1.7m»
A sun, partial shade
S fertile light loam
pH neutral
H upright
! always cook fruit

Galium odoratum
Sweet Woodruff

H6 *Rubiaceae family.* Clusters of small star shaped white flowers. Aromatic, narrow, lance-shaped leaves, 6–8 leaves grow around each stem in a complete circle. Use young leaves in salads.

herbaceous perennial
^15cm «indefinite»
A sun, partial shade
S light loam
pH universal
H mat forming, creeping
! do not take in excess

Ginkgo biloba
Gingko, Maidenhair Tree

H6 *Gingoaceae family.* This herb is dioecious. Flowers on the female tree are followed by small fruit. The leaves are mid-green & blade-shaped with a slit in the centre. Fruit must be cooked.

deciduous tree
^up to 40m «up to 20m»
A full sun
S light loam, free draining
pH universal
H tree
! do not take in excess

14

Glycyrrhiza glabra
Liquorice

H6 *Papilionaceae family.* Pale blue/violet pea-like flowers. The large green leaves are divided into oval leaflets. Root is used to flavour drinks & sauces. Important Chinese medicinal herb.

herbaceous perennial
^1.5m «1–2m»
A sun, partial shade
S fertile loam
pH universal
H upright, creeping
! do not self-medicate

7

Gynostemma pentaphyllum
Sweet Tea Vine, Jiaogulan

H5 *Cucurbitaceae family.* This herb is dioecious. Pale yellow flowers with small palmate, glossy, serrated green leaves. Leaves have a sweet cucumber flavour, use to make tisanes.

herbaceous perennial
  vine
^up to 8m «up to 2m»
A sun, partial shade
S fertile loam
pH universal
H climber

Helichrysum italicum 'Korma'
Curry Plant Korma

H4 *Asteraceae family.* Tiny mustard yellow flowers in domed clusters. Very silver narrow leaves which smell of curry. Use the leaves sparingly, they do not taste as good as they smell.

evergreen shrub
^60cm «1m»
A full sun
S light loam,
  free draining
pH universal
H bushy

Hesperis matronalis
Sweet Rocket

H5 *Asteraceae family.* Clusters of night-scented white or purple flowers. Grey/green, hairy, lance-shaped leaves. Good food plant for the Orange-tip butterfly. Edible flowers.

perennial
^90cm «45cm»
A sun, partial shade
S chalk, light loam
pH universal
H upright

Houttuynia cordata
Fish Mint, Fish Wort

H6 *Saururaceae family.* Dense spikes of white flowers. Blue/green, heart-shaped leaves. Young leaves are edible & have a fishy flavour. Roots are eaten in China as a vegetable. Medicinal herb.

herbaceous perennial
^30cm «1m»
A sun, partial shade
S clay, loam
pH universal
H mat forming, creeping
! do not use if pregnant,
  invasive

Humulus lupulus
Hop

H6   *Cannabaceae family.* This herb is dioecious with pale green flowers. The female flower is cone-like & hidden by paper-like scales. Green leaves have 3–5 lobes with sharp, toothed edges.

herbaceous perennial
  vine
^up to 9m «1.5m»
A sun, partial shade
S light loam, sand
pH universal
H climber
! can cause dermatitis

Humulus lupulus 'Aureus'
Golden Hop

H6   *Cannabaceae family.* This herb is dioecious. Female flower is cone-like & hidden by paper-like scales. Golden leaves have 3–5 lobes with sharp, toothed edges; can be prone to sun scorch.

herbaceous perennial
  vine
^up to 9m «1.5m»
A sun, partial shade
S light loam, sand
pH universal
H climber
! can cause dermatitis

Hypericum perforatum
St John's Wort

H6   *Clusiaceae family.* Lightly scented yellow flowers with tiny black gland dots. Small stalkless, oval, green leaves, covered with tiny translucent resin glands that look like small spots.

semi-evergreen perennial
^30–90cm «30cm»
A sun, partial shade
S chalk, clay, loam, sand
pH universal
H upright
! do not self medicate,
  poisons livestock

Hyssopus officinalis
Hyssop, Blue Hyssop

H5

Lamiaceae family. Dense spikes of small dark blue/violet flowers. Small, narrow, lance-shaped, aromatic, green leaves. Flowers & leaves are edible. Leaves have a strong bitter minty flavour.

semi-evergreen perennial
^80cm «90cm»
A full sun
S light loam, free draining
pH neutral–alkaline
H bushy
! do not self-medicate

Hyssopus officinalis f. *albus*
White Hyssop

H5

Lamiaceae family. Dense spikes of small white flowers. Small, narrow, lance-shaped, aromatic, green leaves. Flowers & leaves are edible; use small amounts with fatty fish & meat.

semi-evergreen perennial
^80cm «90cm»
A full sun
S light loam, free draining
pH neutral–alkaline
H bushy
! do not self-medicate

Hyssopus officinalis subsp. *aristatus*
Rock Hyssop

H5

Lamiaceae family. Dense spikes of small dark blue flowers. Small, narrow, lance-shaped, aromatic, green leaves. Good compact habit. Add leaves to soups, stews & fatty food.

semi-evergreen perennial
^30cm «45cm»
A full sun
S chalk, loam, sand,
  free draining
pH neutral–alkaline
H bushy
! do not self-medicate

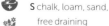

Hyssopus officinalis 'Roseus'
Pink Hyssop

H5 *Lamiaceae family.* Dense spikes of small sugar pink flowers. Small, narrow, lance-shaped, aromatic, green leaves. Flowers & leaves are edible; use small amounts with fatty fish & meat.

semi-evergreen perennial
^80cm «90cm»
A full sun
S light loam, free draining
pH neutral–alkaline
H bushy
! do not self-medicate

Istatis tinctoria
Woad

H4 *Brassicaceae family.* Clusters of small bright yellow, sweetly scented flowers in 2nd season followed by pendulous brown/black seeds. Lance-shaped, toothed, blue/green leaves.

perennial
^up to 1.3m «45cm»
A sun
S light loam, free draining
pH neutral–alkaline
H upright
! do not self-medicate

Jasminum officinale
Jasmine, Common Jasmine

H5 *Oleaceae family.* Small fragrant white flowers, followed by black berries. Pinnate leaves which have 3–9 leaflets. Edible flowers, great in drinks & puddings.

shrub, deciduous climber
^up to 8m «up to 2.5m»
A sun
S loam, free draining
pH acid–neutral
H climber
! poisonous berries, do not ingest essential oil

Laurus nobilis
Bay

H4 *Lauraceae family.* Small pale yellow flowers, followed by oval berries, black when ripe. Oval, dark green leaves, with a shiny upper surface. Use leaves with milk dishes, stews & soups.

evergreen tree
^up to 8m «up to 3m»
A full sun
S loam
pH acid–neutral
H bushy

Lavandula angustifolia See pages 60–61

Lavandula 'Bee Happy'
Lavender Bee Happy

H3 *Lamiaceae family.* Oblong flower head covered in small blue flowers topped with white bracts. Narrow, short, green grey aromatic leaves. Add flowers & bracts to salads.

evergreen shrub
^45cm «50cm»
A full sun
S chalk, loam, sand, free draining
pH universal
H bushy

Lavandula x *chaytoriae* 'Sawyers'
Lavender Sawyers

H4 *Lamiaceae family.* Conical spikes of pale purple flowers. Soft, linear, silver grey, aromatic leaves. The flowers can be added to drinks, pastries & puddings.

evergreen shrub
^60cm «60cm»
A full sun
S chalk, loam, sand, free draining
pH universal
H bushy

Lavandula x *christiana*
Lavender Christiana

H1c   *Lamiaceae family.* Blue trident flowers all year round. Serrated, aromatic, silver foliage. Very attractive plant, needs protection in winter from frost & rain. Add the flowers to ice cubes.

evergreen shrub
^75cm «75cm»
A full sun
S chalk, loam, sand,
   free draining
pH universal
H bushy

Lavandula dentata
Fringed Lavender, Lavender Dentata

H3   *Lamiaceae family.* Oblong flower head covered in pale mauve flowers topped with short pale mauve bracts. Deeply serrated highly aromatic green leaves that smell strongly of eucalyptus.

evergreen shrub
^50cm «50cm»
A full sun
S chalk, loam, sand,
   free draining
pH universal
H bushy

Lavandula dentata var. *candicans*
Lavender Candicans

H2 *Lamiaceae family.* Oblong flower head covered in pale purple flowers, topped with short pale purple bracts. Serrated soft grey leaves. Flowers & bracts can be added to salads.

evergreen shrub
^75cm «75cm»
A full sun
S chalk, loam, sand,
   free draining
pH universal
H bushy

Lavandula angustifolia

H5 *Lamiaceae family.* This group of lavenders is tough, hardy & very popular. They are renowned for making lavender hedges as they have a compact habit with narrow grey, green aromatic leaves to which the epithet *angustifolia* (meaning narrow leaves) refers. They are all evergreen shrubs, height 30–60cm, spread 30–60cm, with short compact spikes of interrupted small flowers that vary in colour from white & pink, to purple, violet & blue. Add flowers & leaves sparingly to stews & use to flavour sugar for use in puddings & baking.

evergreen shrub
^30–60cm «30–60»
A full sun
S chalk, loam, sand, free draining
pH universal
H bushy

Lavandula angustifolia 'Folgate'
Lavender Folgate

Short spikes of mid purple blue flowers.

^60cm «60cm»

Lavandula angustifolia 'Hidcote'
Lavender Hidcote

Short spikes of dark violet flowers.

^50cm «50cm»

Lavandula angustifolia 'Miss Muffett'
Lavender Miss Muffett

Short spikes of
mauve flowers.

^30cm «30cm»

Lavandula angustifolia 'Munstead'
Lavender Munstead

Short spikes of mid-
blue flowers.

^45cm «45cm»

Lavandula angustifolia 'Rosea'
Lavender Rosea

Short spikes of pale
pink flowers.

^45cm «45cm»

Lavandula angustifolia 'Twickel Purple'
Lavender Twickel Purple

Medium spikes of
mauve flowers.

^45cm «45cm»

Lavandula x intermedia

H5 *Lamiaceae family.* These large elegant lavenders are a cross between *angustifolia* subsp. *angustifolia* (meaning narrow leaves) & *latifolia* (meaning broad leaves) & are often called Lavandin. They look beautiful as specimens in the garden or as large hedges. They have long spikes of small flowers that vary in colour from white & pink to purple, violet & blue. Narrow, lance-shaped to almost spoon-shaped grey, green, aromatic, leaves. Evergreen shrubs, height 75cm–1m & spread 75cm–1m. Add flowers & leaves sparingly to stews & to flavour sugar for use in puddings or for baking.

evergreen shrub
^75cm–1m «75cm–1m»
A full sun
S chalk, loam, sand, free draining
pH universal
H bushy

Lavandula x intermedia 'Edelweiss'
Lavender Edelweiss

Very long spikes of white flowers.

^85cm «75cm»

Lavandula x intermedia 'Grosso'
Lavender Grosso

Very long spikes of purple blue flowers.

^85cm «65cm»

Lavandula x *intermedia* 'Lullingstone Castle'
Lavender Lullingstone Castle

Long spikes of
mauve flowers.

^1m «1m»

Lavandula x *intermedia* Old English Group
Lavender Old English

Aromatic, long
pointed spikes of
clear pale blue/
purple flowers.

^90cm «90cm»

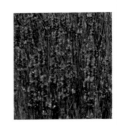

Lavandula x *intermedia* 'Pale Pretender'
Lavender Pale Pretender

Long spikes of pale
mauve flowers.

^85cm «85cm»

Lavandula x *intermedia* 'Seal'
Lavender Seal

Long spikes of pale
purple flowers.

^1m «1m»

Lavandula 'Fathead'
Lavender Fathead

H3 *Lamiaceae family.* A round flower head of small deep purple flowers topped with pale mauve bracts. Narrow, short, green grey aromatic leaves. Add flowers & bracts to salads.

evergreen shrub
^45cm «50cm»
A full sun
S chalk, loam, sand, free draining
pH universal
H bushy

Lavandula x ginginsii 'Goodwin Creek Grey'
Lavender Goodwin Creek Grey

H2 *Lamiaceae family.* Very long blue purple flower spikes. Broad, toothed, velvety, grey/green leaves. Edible flowers, use in sweet & savoury salads & also with puddings.

evergreen shrub
^75cm «75cm»
A full sun
S chalk, loam, sand, free draining
pH universal
H bushy

Lavandula x intermedia *See pages 62–63*

Lavandula lanata
Woolly Lavender

H4 *Lamiaceae family.* Medium spikes of attractive dark purple flowers. Lovely soft, silver grey, aromatic foliage. Flowers can be added to drinks, pastries & puddings.

evergreen shrub
^50cm «50cm»
A full sun
S chalk, loam, sand, free draining
pH universal
H bushy

Lavandula pedunculata
Portuguese Lavender

H3 *Lamiaceae family.* Oblong flower head covered in purple flowers with long mauve bracts in summer. Narrow, short, grey/green aromatic leaves. Add flowers & bracts to drinks, pastries & puddings.

evergreen shrub
^60cm «60cm»
A full sun
S chalk, loam, sand, free draining
pH acid–neutral
H bushy

Lavandula stoechas
French Lavender

H3 *Lamiaceae family.* Oblong flower head covered in purple flowers & pale mauve bracts. Short, narrow, grey/green aromatic leaves. Add flowers & bracts to drinks, pastries & puddings.

evergreen shrub
^45cm «45cm»
A full sun
S chalk, loam, sand, free draining
pH acid–neutral
H bushy

Lavandula stoechas subsp. *stoechas* f. *rosea* 'Kew Red'   Lavender Kew Red

H3 *Lamiaceae family.* Oblong flower head covered in crimson flowers topped with pale pink bracts. Narrow, short, grey/green aromatic leaves. Add flowers & bracts to drinks, pastries & puddings.

evergreen shrub
^40cm «40cm»
A full sun
S chalk, loam, sand, free draining
pH acid–neutral
H bushy

Lavandula viridis
Green Lavender, Lemon Lavender

H3 *Lamiaceae family.* Oblong flower heads covered in lime green flowers topped with pale green bracts. Linear, sticky green leaves. Pine, lemon, lavender scent to flowers & leaves.

evergreen shrub
^60cm «60cm»
A full sun
S chalk, loam, sand,
   free draining
pH universal
H bushy

Lavandula viridis 'Jekka's Blue'
Lavender Jekka's Blue

H3 *Lamiaceae family.* Oblong flower heads covered in pale blue flowers topped with pale green bracts. Linear, sticky green leaves. Pine, lemon, lavender scent to flowers & leaves.

evergreen shrub
^60cm «60cm»
A full sun
S chalk, loam, sand,
   free draining
pH universal
H bushy

Lavandula 'Willow Vale'
Lavender Willow Vale

H3 *Lamiaceae family.* Large oblong flower head with dark purple flowers topped with large purple bracts. Narrow, short, aromatic, grey/green leaves. Add flowers & bracts to drinks.

evergreen shrub
^60cm «60cm»
A full sun
S chalk, loam, sand,
   free draining
pH universal
H bushy

Lepechina hastata
False Salvia, Pitcher Sage

H4 *Lamiaceae family.* Spikes of dark magenta
 flowers. Large, aromatic, grey/green leaves. In
 warm climates this is an evergreen. Only the
 flowers are edible, use in salads & ice cubes.

 evergreen shrub
^up to 1.2m «60cm»
A full sun
S light loam,
   free draining
pH neutral
H upright

Leptospermum scoparium
New Zealand Tea Tree

H4 *Myrtaceae family.* Beautiful 5-petalled white
 flowers followed by brown seed heads. Small,
 grey/green leaves that become prickly as they
mature. Flowers are known for Manuka honey.

evergreen tree
^up to 2.5m «up to 2.5m»
A full sun
S light loam,
   free draining
pH acid–neutral
H bushy

Levisticum officinale
Lovage

H5 *Apiaceae family.* Clusters of tiny yellow/pale
 green flowers, followed by brown seeds. Divided
 toothed leaves, celery-scented when crushed.
 Seeds, flowers & leaves taste of meaty celery.

 herbaceous perennial
^up to 2m «1m»
A full sun
S fertile loam
 pH neutral
 H upright
 ! do not self-medicate

Ligusticum scoticum
Scottish Lovage

H5 *Apiaceae family.* Umbels of white flowers, followed by edible seeds. Glossy leaves divided into 3 broad, toothed leaflets on red green stems. Flowers & seeds are edible. Use sparingly.

herbaceous perennial
^up to 90cm «75cm»
A full sun
S loam, free draining
pH universal
H upright

Linum perenne
Flax, Linseed

H4 *Linaceae family.* Sky blue flowers. Small, narrow, mid-green leaves. The seeds are used in breads, baking & cereals.

herbaceous perennial
^60cm «30cm»
A full sun
S loam, free draining
pH universal
H upright, arching
! seeds may be
   poisonous to livestock

Lippia dulcis
Aztec Sweet Herb

H2 *Verbenaceae family.* Beautiful cone-shaped white flowers. The small green leaves can have a purple tinge if the night temperature dips below 3°C. Use leaves to sweeten fruit dishes.

partial evergreen
^30cm «indefinite»
A full sun
S light loam,
   free draining
pH universal
H mat forming

Luma apiculata
Luma Arrayan

H4 *Myrtaceae family.* Pretty small white flowers
with golden stamens, followed by round purple
berries. Aromatic, dark green leaves. Wonderful
orange bark. Use berries to make sauces & jams.

evergreen shrub
^up to 10m «up to 5m»
A sun, partial shade
S chalk, clay, loam, sand
pH universal
H bushy
! always cook berries

Luma apiculata 'Glanleam Gold' (v)
Luma Glanleam Gold

H4 *Myrtaceae family.* Pretty small white flowers
with golden stamens, followed by round purple
berries. Aromatic, variegated gold/cream/green
leaves. Use berries to make sauces & jams.

evergreen shrub
^up to 3m «up to 2m»
A sun, partial shade
S chalk, clay, loam, sand
pH universal
H bushy
! always cook berries

Luma apiculata 'Nana'
Dwarf Luma

H4 *Myrtaceae family.* Small fragrant white flowers,
followed by round purple berries. Small dark
green leaves. The berries are used to make
sauces & jams. Ideal container plant.

evergreen shrub
^60cm «60cm»
A sun, partial shade
S chalk, clay, loam, sand
pH universal
H bushy
! always cook berries

Luma apiculata 'Penlee' (v)
Luma 'Penlee'

H4 *Myrtaceae family.* Pretty small white flowers with golden stamens, followed by round purple berries. Variegated grey/green/cream leaves. Use berries to make sauces & jams.

evergreen shrub
^up to 3m «up to 2m»
A sun, partial shade
S chalk, clay, loam, sand
pH universal
H bushy
! always cook berries

Luma apiculata 'St Hilary' (v)
Luma 'St Hilary'

H4 *Myrtaceae family.* Small white flowers with golden stamens, followed by purple berries. Variegated grey/green/cream leaves. Stems are deep maroon when young. Use berries to make sauces & jams.

evergreen shrub
^up to 3m «up to 2m»
A sun, partial shade
S chalk, clay, loam, sand
pH universal
H bushy
! always cook berries

Luma chequen
Chilean Luma, Chilean Myrtle

H4 *Myrtaceae family.* White flowers followed by dark blue/purple berries. Aromatic, dark green, oval leaves with a slight point, with a lighter green underside. Use fruit for sauces & jellies.

evergreen tree
^up to 15m «up to 6m»
A sun, partial shade
S chalk, clay, loam, sand
pH universal
H bushy
! always cook berries

Malva moschata
Musk Mallow

H5 *Malvaceae family*. Pretty white/pink, lightly scented flowers. Feathery, musk-scented, kidney-shaped, green leaves. Young leaves are often added to wild salads, an acquired taste!

herbaceous perennial
^up to 80cm
 «up to 60cm»
A full sun
S chalk, clay, loam, sand
pH universal
H upright

Malva sylvestris
Common Mallow

H5 *Malvaceae family*. Pretty pale purple/pink flowers which have dark-coloured veins. Mid-green, rounded, ivy-shaped leaves. Young leaves can be used in salads.

herbaceous perennial
^up to 90cm
 «up to 60cm»
A full sun
S chalk, clay, loam, sand
pH universal
H upright

Mandragora officinarum
Mandrake

H4 *Solanaceae family*. Small bell-shaped white/blue flowers followed, in warm climates, by round yellow fruits in late summer. Large oval green leaves, have a rough, slightly prickly texture.

herbaceous perennial
^5cm «30cm»
A sun, partial shade
S chalk, loam, sand,
 free draining
pH acid–neutral
H upright
! do not self-medicate

Marrubium vulgare
White Horehound

H5 *Lamiaceae family.* Small creamy white flowers from the 2nd season. Aromatic, green, oval, wrinkled, lightly toothed leaves with woolly silky silver underside. Used in traditional ale brewing.

herbaceous perennial
^45cm «30cm»
A full sun
S chalk, loam, sand, free draining
pH universal
H upright
! do not self-medicate

Melissa officinalis
Lemon Balm

H5 *Lamiaceae family.* Clusters of small pale creamy flowers. Lemon-scented, oval, toothed, textured, green leaves. Use with fruit, chicken & eggs. Leaves make a very refreshing tisane.

herbaceous perennial
^up to 75cm «45cm»
A full sun
S chalk, loam, sand, free draining
pH universal
H bushy

Melissa officinalis 'All Gold'
Lemon Balm All Gold

H5 *Lamiaceae family.* Clusters of small pale creamy flowers. Lemon-scented, oval, toothed, textured, golden leaves which will scorch in full sun. Use with fruit, chicken, eggs & salad dishes.

herbaceous perennial
^up to 50cm «30cm»
A full sun
S chalk, loam, sand, free draining
pH universal
H bushy

Melissa officinalis 'Aurea'
Variegated Lemon Balm

H5 *Lamiaceae family.* Clusters of small pale creamy flowers. Lemon-scented, oval, toothed, textured, variegated gold/green leaves. Use with fruit, chicken & egg dishes.

herbaceous perennial
^up to 65cm «45cm»
A full sun
S chalk, loam, sand,
   free draining
pH universal
H bushy

Mentha arvensis 'Banana'
Banana Mint

H5 *Lamiaceae family.* Pale lilac flowers in whorls down the stem. Bright green, small leaves, peppermint, with hint of banana, scented. Use leaves & flowers in summer drinks & fruit dishes.

herbaceous perennial
^30cm «indefinite»
A full sun
S chalk, loam, sand,
   free draining
pH universal
H upright, creeping

Mentha arvensis var. *piperascens*
Japanese Mint

H5 *Lamiaceae family.* Terminal tight oval clusters of lilac flowers. Bright green, round, peppermint-scented leaves. Flowers & leaves are edible. Use leaves to make a strong peppermint tea.

herbaceous perennial
^60cm «indefinite»
A full sun
S chalk, loam, sand,
   free draining
pH universal
H upright, creeping
! do not self-medicate

Mentha 'Berries and Cream'
Berries and Cream Mint

 H5   *Lamiaceae family.* Attractive tight, terminal clusters of mauve flowers. Dark green, peppermint/fruity-scented leaves. Use leaves & flowers in summer drinks.

 herbaceous perennial

^45cm «indefinite»

A full sun

S chalk, loam, sand, free draining

pH universal

H upright, creeping

Mentha cervina
Harts Pennyroyal

 H5   *Lamiaceae family.* Small mauve flowers in whorls around the stem. Narrow, mid-green, peppermint-scented leaves. Rub crushed leaves onto insect bites to reduce swelling. Flowers are edible.

 herbaceous perennial

^20cm «indefinite»

A sun, partial shade

S chalk, loam, sand

pH universal

H mat forming, creeping

! do not self-medicate

Mentha cervina alba
White Harts Pennyroyal

 H5   *Lamiaceae family.* Small white flowers in whorls around the stem. Narrow, mid-green, peppermint-scented leaves. Rub crushed leaves onto insect bites to reduce swelling. Flowers are edible.

 herbaceous perennial

^20cm «indefinite»

A sun, partial shade

S chalk, loam, sand

pH universal

H mat forming, creeping

! do not self-medicate

Mentha x *gracilis* 'Variegata' (v)
Ginger Mint

H5 *Lamiaceae family.* Clusters of mauve flowers in tight whorls around the stem. Oval, pointed, variegated gold & green leaves. Flowers & leaves are edible. Add to vegetables & salads.

herbaceous perennial
^50cm «indefinite»
A full sun
S chalk, loam, sand, free draining
pH universal
H upright, creeping

Mentha lavender mint
Lavender Mint

H5 *Lamiaceae family.* Tight cluster of pink/mauve flowers. Dark green leaves with hints of purple & orange with lavender scent. Flowers & leaves are edible. Use leaves for flavouring vinegars.

herbaceous perennial
^80cm «indefinite»
A full sun
S chalk, loam, sand, free draining
pH universal
H upright, creeping

Mentha longifolia Buddleia Mint Group
Buddleia Mint

H6 *Lamiaceae family.* Long terminal cones of mauve flowers. Long oval grey, green, toothed leaves. Great for flower arranging. The flowers are edible.

herbaceous perennial
^90cm «indefinite»
A full sun
S chalk, loam, sand, free draining
pH universal
H upright, creeping

Mentha longifolia 'Buddleia Mint Group variegated' (v)   Variegated Buddleia Mint

H5 *Lamiaceae family.* Long terminal cones of pale mauve flowers. Grey, variegated with cream, yellow & green, oval, toothed leaves. Great for flower arranging. Flowers are edible.

herbaceous perennial
^45cm «indefinite»
A full sun
S chalk, loam, sand, free draining
pH universal
H upright, creeping

Mentha longifolia subsp. *schimperi*
Desert Mint

H4 *Lamiaceae family.* Very long terminal of pale mauve flowers. Long thin grey leaves which have a strong peppermint flavour. The leaves are used to make the traditional Moroccan tea.

herbaceous perennial
^90cm «indefinite»
A full sun
S chalk, loam, sand, free draining
pH universal
H upright, creeping

Mentha longifolia 'Silver Leaved'
Silver Mint

H5 *Lamiaceae family.* Short terminal cones of pale mauve flowers. Soft, narrow, lance-shaped, hairy, silver leaves. Good for flower arrangements. Flowers are edible.

herbaceous perennial
^60cm «indefinite»
A full sun
S chalk, loam, sand, free draining
pH universal
H upright, creeping

Mentha x piperata See pages 78–79

Mentha pulegium 'Cunningham Mint'
Creeping Pennyroyal

H6 *Lamiaceae family*. Small mauve flowers in
terminal, globular clusters, very rarely flowers.
Peppermint-scented, small oval leaves. Rub
leaves onto insect bites to reduce swelling.

semi-evergreen perennial
^3cm «up to 60cm»
A sun, partial shade
S chalk, loam, sand
pH universal
H mat forming, creeping
! do not self-medicate

Mentha pulegium 'Upright'
Upright Pennyroyal

H6 *Lamiaceae family*. Small mauve flowers in
terminal, globular clusters in summer. Small
oval, peppermint-scented leaves. Rub crushed
leaves onto insect bites to reduce swelling.

semi-evergreen perennial
^15cm «up to 60cm»
A sun, partial shade
S chalk, loam, sand
pH universal
H mat forming, creeping
! do not self-medicate

Mentha requienii
Corsican Mint

H5 *Lamiaceae family*. Tiny purple flowers &
peppermint-scented leaves which look like
thyme until you touch them. Good for herb seats
& for occasional walking on. Flowers are edible.

semi-evergreen perennial
^½cm «up to 60cm»
A full sun
S chalk, loam, sand
pH universal
H mat forming, creeping

Mentha x piperita

H5

Lamiaceae family. Peppermint has a much more pungent flavour than spearmint; it is used in many products including medicines & toothpaste. It is a herbaceous perennial, height 40–80cm, spread indefinite with small pink to pale purple flowers in terminal, cylindrical spikes. Pointed, oval, occasionally round, toothed, peppermint-scented & flavoured leaves. Leaves vary in colour from dark brown to mid-green. Flowers & leaves are edible. Use leaves in puddings, cakes, oils, vinegars & for making hot or cold tisanes.

herbaceous perennial
^40–80cm «indefinite»
A full sun
S chalk, loam, sand, free draining
pH universal
H upright, creeping

Mentha x piperita
Peppermint

Small pale purple flowers. Mid-green leaves, tinged with brown along the veins.

 ^50cm «indefinite»

Mentha x piperita 'Black Mitcham'
Black Mitcham Mint

Small pale purple flowers. Dark brown leaves, tinged with green.

 ^60cm «indefinite»

Mentha x *piperita* f. *citrata*
Eau de Cologne Mint

Tight clusters of small mauve flowers both terminal & as a whorl around the stem. Dark brown leaves, tinged with green. Add leaves to bathwater.

 ^80cm «indefinite»

Mentha x *piperita* f. *citrata* 'Basil'
Basil Mint

Tight clusters of purple flowers both terminal & as a whorl around the stem. Mid-green leaves. Use as a substitute for basil in early spring.

^45cm «indefinite»

Mentha x *piperita* f. *citrata* 'Chocolate'
Chocolate Mint

Tight clusters of small mauve flowers both terminal & as a whorl around the stem. Dark green leaves. Great in puddings.

^60cm «indefinite»

Mentha x *piperita* f. *citrata* 'Orange'
Orange Mint

Mauve/pink flowers, summer to autumn. Round purple & orange-tinged, dark green leaves. Orange flavour. Good in salads, both fruit & savoury.

^80cm «indefinite»

Mentha spicata

Lamiaceae family. Spearmint is the quintessential mint & it can be found growing throughout the world. The leaf flavour is warm & sweet with light menthol notes. It is a herbaceous perennial, height 40–60cm & spread indefinite, with small flowers in terminal, cylindrical, spikes that vary in colour from white to mauve. Mid-green, mint-scented & flavoured, lanced, oval-shaped wrinkled leaves. Flowers & leaves are edible. Great with potatoes & for sauces, especially mint sauces. Leaves make a lovely refreshing mint tea, either hot or cold.

herbaceous perennial
^40–80cm «indefinite»
A full sun
S chalk, loam, sand, free draining
pH universal
H upright, creeping

Mentha spicata
Spearmint, Garden Mint

H6 Small purple/mauve flowers.

^60cm «indefinite»

Mentha spicata var. crispa
Curly Mint

H6 Small lilac/pink flowers.

^60cm «indefinite»

Mentha spicata var. *crispa* 'Moroccan'
Moroccan Mint

H6   Small white flowers.

^60cm «indefinite»

Mentha spicata 'Spanish Pointed'
Spanish Mint

H5   Small mauve flowers.

^50cm «indefinite»

Mentha spicata 'Stavordale'
Stavordale Mint

H6   Small purple/mauve flowers.

^60cm «indefinite»

Mentha spicata 'Tashkent'
Tashkent Mint

H6   Small mauve flowers.

^80cm «indefinite»

Mentha sativa
Traditional Garden Mint

H6 *Lamiaceae family.* Small mauve flowers in terminal, cylindrical spikes. Bright mid-green, oval-shaped, wrinkled, spearmint-scented & flavoured leaves. Use for sauces & mint teas.

herbaceous perennial
^60cm «indefinite»
A full sun
S chalk, loam, sand, free draining
pH universal
H upright, creeping

Mentha x *smithiana*
Red Mint

H5 *Lamiaceae family.* Clusters of small mauve flowers both terminal & as a whorl around the stem. Oval, pointed, mid-green leaves with purple/red hue. The stem is red. Use in sauces & jams.

herbaceous perennial
^45cm «indefinite»
A full sun
S chalk, loam, sand, free draining
pH universal
H upright, creeping

Mentha spicata See pages 80–81

Mentha suaveolens
Apple Mint

H6 *Lamiaceae family.* Tight terminal oval clusters of mauve flowers. Oval, hairy, mid-green leaves. Flowers & leaves are edible. Use leaves for mint sauces & jellies. Add chopped leaves to salads.

herbaceous perennial
^80cm «indefinite»
A full sun
S chalk, loam, sand, free draining
pH universal
H upright, creeping

Mentha suaveolens 'Pineapple'
Pineapple Mint

H5 *Lamiaceae family.* Tight terminal oval clusters of white flowers. Oval, hairy, variegated mid-green & white leaves. Flowers & leaves are edible. The leaves are good for mint sauces & jellies.

herbaceous perennial
^60cm «indefinite»
A full sun
S chalk, loam, sand,
  free draining
pH universal
H upright, creeping

Mentha suaveolens subsp. *timija*
Atlas Mountains Mint

H5 *Lamiaceae family.* Tight terminal oval clusters of mauve flowers. Small oval, hairy, grey/green leaves. Flowers & leaves are edible. The leaves taste better when cooked.

herbaceous perennial
^60cm «indefinite»
A full sun
S chalk, loam, sand,
  free draining
pH universal
H upright, creeping

Mentha x *villosa* var. *alopecuroides*
'Bowles's Mint'   Bowles's Mint

H5 *Lamiaceae family.* Small pale mauve flowers in terminal cylindrical spikes. Large, round, hairy, leaves, with a unique flavour (mix of peppermint & spearmint). Leaves make a great mint sauce.

herbaceous perennial
^up to 1m «indefinite»
A full sun
S chalk, loam, sand,
  free draining
pH universal
H upright, creeping

Meum athamanticum
Meu, Spignel

H6 *Apiaceae family.* Umbels of small white flowers with a hint of pink around the edges of the cluster. Feathery, soft, spicy-scented, bright green leaves. Young leaves & roots are edible.

herbaceous perennial
^30cm «20cm»
A sun, partial shade
S loam, sand,
   free draining
pH neutral–alkaline
H clump

Micromeria fruticosa
Mediterranean Rock Mint

H3 *Lamiaceae family.* Small white flowers. Small oval, silvery green leaves with a minty marjoram flavour. Used in Middle Eastern cooking, good with tomatoes, lamb & mushrooms.

herbaceous perennial
^40cm «40cm»
A full sun
S light loam,
   free draining
pH universal
H bushy

Micromeria subsp.
Emperor's Mint

H4 *Lamiaceae family.* Small pale pink/white flowers in summer. Small roundish, grey/green, aromatic leaves. The leaves have a strong minty flavour, good for use in cooking & teas.

herbaceous perennial
^25cm «40cm»
A full sun
S light loam,
   free draining
pH universal
H bushy

Monarda citriodora
Lemon Bergamot, Lemon Bee Balm

H3 *Lamiaceae family.* Beautiful lilac flowers
with mauve bracts with a pink tinge. Lemon-
scented, bright green, toothed, slightly hairy
green leaves. Flower petals & leaves are edible.

annual
^up to 1.2m «45cm»
A sun, partial shade
S loam, free draining
pH universal
H upright

Monarda didyma
Bee Balm Bergamot, Red Bergamot

H5 *Lamiaceae family.* Large red flowers in dense
terminal whorls. Mid-green, lanced-shaped,
toothed, pointed, strongly scented leaves. Flower
petals & leaves are edible. Use leaves sparingly.

herbaceous perennial
^up to 80cm «45cm»
A sun, partial shade
S loam, free draining
pH universal
H upright

Monarda fistulosa
Wild Bergamot

H5 *Lamiaceae family.* Lilac flowers with mauve bracts
with a pink tinge. Aromatic, slightly toothed, hairy
green leaves. Petals & leaves are edible. Use leaves
sparingly; they are good for tea.

herbaceous perennial
^up to 1.2m «45cm»
A sun, partial shade
S loam, free draining
pH universal
H upright

Myrrhis odorata
Sweet Cicely

H5 *Apiaceae family.* Flat umbels of sweetly scented white flowers, followed by long seeds that ripen to black. Leaves are divided & smell of sweet aniseed. Flowers, seeds, leaves & roots are edible.

herbaceous perennial
^up to 90cm «60cm»
A sun, partial shade
S damp loam
pH universal
H clump

Myrtus communis
Myrtle

H4 *Myrtaceae family.* Small white flowers with golden stamens, followed by blue/black berries in autumn. Dark green, shiny oval, aromatic leaves. Use the berries to make gin.

evergreen shrub
^up to 3m «up to 3m»
A full sun
S light loam,
    free draining
pH universal
H bushy

Myrtus communis 'Jekka's All Gold'
Myrtle Jekka's All Gold

H3 *Myrtaceae family.* White flowers with a hint of pink, followed by blue/black berries. Oval, light green & yellow variegated, aromatic leaves. Berries & leaves can be used in cooking.

evergreen shrub
^up to 2m «up to 2m»
A full sun
S light loam,
    free draining
pH universal
H bushy

Myrtus communis 'Merion'
Merion Myrtle

H3   *Myrtaceae family.* Fragrant white flowers with golden stamens, followed by black/blue berries. Small oval, pointed, aromatic, dark green leaves. Use leaves as a flavouring.

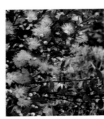

evergreen shrub
^up to 2m «up to 2m»
A full sun
S light loam,
    free draining
pH universal
H bushy

Myrtus communis 'Pyewood Park'
Pyewood Park Myrtle

H3 *Myrtaceae family.* Fragrant white flowers with golden stamens, followed by black/blue berries. Oval, pointed, aromatic, dark green leaves. Use leaves to flavour roasts & soups.

evergreen shrub
^up to 2m «up to 2m»
A full sun
S light loam,
    free draining
pH universal
H bushy

Myrtus communis subsp. *tarentina*
Tarentina Myrtle

H4 *Myrtaceae family.* Small white flowers with golden stamens, followed by blue/black berries. Small, oval, pointed, shiny, dark green, aromatic leaves. Berries & leaves can be used in cooking.

evergreen shrub
^up to 2m «up to 2m»
A full sun
S light loam,
    free draining
pH universal
H bushy

Myrtus communis subsp. *tarentina* 'Microphylla Variegata' (v)
Variegated Tarentina Myrtle

H3 *Myrtaceae family.* Fragrant white flowers with golden stamens, followed by black/blue berries. Small oval, aromatic, light green & white variegated leaves. Use leaves to flavour roast dishes.

evergreen shrub
^up to 1m «up to 1m»
A full sun
S light loam, free draining
pH universal
H bushy

Myrtus communis 'Variegata' (v)
Variegated Myrtle

H4 *Myrtaceae family.* White flowers with a hint of pink, followed by blue/black berries. Oval, light green & cream variegated, aromatic leaves. Berries & leaves can be used in cooking.

evergreen shrub
^up to 2m «up to 2m»
A full sun
S light loam,
   free draining
pH universal
H bushy

Nepeta cataria
Catnep, Catnip

H5 *Lamiaceae family.* Clusters of small pale pinkish white tubular flowers. Pungent, aromatic grey/green, toothed, oval leaves. Leaves & flowers are edible. Leaves are good in stuffings & marinades.

herbaceous perennial
^up to 1m «60cm»
A full sun
S chalk, loam, sand,
   free draining
pH universal
H upright

Nepeta cataria 'Citriodora'
Lemon Scented Catnip

H5 *Lamiaceae family.* Clusters of small pale pink/white tubular flowers. Pungent, aromatic, lemon-scented, grey/green, toothed, oval leaves. Leaves & flowers are edible. Leaves are good in stuffings.

herbaceous perennial
^up to 1m «60cm»
A full sun
S chalk, loam, sand, free draining
pH universal
H upright

Nepeta x *faassenii*
Catmint, Catnip

H5 *Lamiaceae family.* Clusters of small lavender blue tubular flowers. Pungent, aromatic, small, grey, toothed, oval leaves. Leaves & flowers are edible. The leaves have a musty mint flavour.

herbaceous perennial
^45cm «45cm»
A full sun
S chalk, loam, sand, free draining
pH universal
H clump

Nepeta x *faassenii* 'Alba'
White Flowering Catmint, Catnip

H5 *Lamiaceae family.* Clusters of small creamy white tubular flowers. Pungent, aromatic, small, grey, toothed, oval leaves. Leaves & flowers are edible. The leaves have a musty mint flavour.

herbaceous perennial
^45cm «45cm»
A full sun
S chalk, loam, sand, free draining
pH universal
H clump

Nepeta racemosa 'Walkers Low'
Catmint Walkers Low

H5 *Lamiaceae family.* Clusters of small sky blue
tubular flowers. Pungent, aromatic, small,
grey, toothed, oval leaves. Leaves & flowers are
edible. The leaves have a musty mint flavour.

herbaceous perennial
^75cm «45cm»
A full sun
S chalk, loam, sand,
free draining
pH universal
H clump, arching

Nepeta 'Six Hills Giant'
Catmint Six Hills Giant

H5 *Lamiaceae family.* Clusters of small lavender
blue tubular flowers. Pungent, aromatic, small,
grey, toothed, oval leaves. Leaves & flowers are
edible. The leaves have a musty mint flavour.

herbaceous perennial
^up to 90cm «45cm»
A full sun
S chalk, loam, sand,
free draining
pH universal
H clump, arching

Ocimum basilicum
Sweet Basil

H1c *Lamiaceae family.* Clusters of small white
tubular flowers that have a lovely sweet basil
flavour. Green, oval, pointed leaves that smell
wonderful when crushed. Leaves are edible.

annual
^45cm «30cm»
A full sun
S loam, sand,
free draining
pH universal
H upright

Ocimum basilicum 'Cinnamon'
Cinnamon Basil

H1c *Lamiaceae family.* Clusters of small pink/mauve tubular flowers. Dark purple/brown stems. Olive green/brown, oval, pointed, slightly serrated, highly aromatic leaves. Leaves are edible.

annual
^45cm «30cm»
A full sun
S loam, sand,
    free draining
pH universal
H upright

Ocimum basilicum 'Horapha Nanum'
Thai Basil, Dwarf Anise

H1c *Lamiaceae family.* Clusters of small purple tubular flowers with dark purple/brown stems. Olive green/purple, oval, pointed, hairy & slightly serrated leaves with a pungent scent & flavour.

annual
^30cm «20cm»
A full sun
S loam, sand,
    free draining
pH universal
H bushy

Ocimum basilicum 'Mrs Burns Lemon'
Mrs Burns Basil, Lemon Basil

H1c *Lamiaceae family.* Clusters of small white flowers. Bright green, oval, pointed, intensely lemon-scented leaves. Use with fish, chicken, rice & pasta, or in salads. Makes a good tisane.

annual
^45cm «20cm»
A full sun
S loam, sand,
    free draining
pH universal
H upright

Ocimum basilicum 'Napolitano'
Lettuce Leaf Basil

H1c   *Lamiaceae family.* Clusters of white flowers. Large, bright green, textured, crinkled oval leaves. Good with pasta, sauces & for making pesto & basil oil.

annual
^50cm «45cm»
A full sun
S loam, sand, free draining
pH universal
H upright

Ocimum basilicum var. *purpurascens* 'Red Rubin'   Red Rubin Basil

H1c   *Lamiaceae family.* Clusters of small pink/mauve tubular flowers. Light purple stems. Dark purple, oval, pointed leaves with a spicy warm flavour. Great added to rice & pastas, or for panna cotta.

annual
^45cm «30cm»
A full sun
S loam, sand, free draining
pH universal
H upright

Ocimum basilicum var. *purpurascens* x *kilimandscharicum*   African Blue Basil

H1c   *Lamiaceae family.* Clusters of small pink/mauve tubular flowers. Dark purple, hairy, oval, pointed leaves with a camphor scent. Plants are used as a fly deterrent. Used with vegetable or meat dishes.

evergreen perennial
^up to 70cm «40cm»
A full sun
S loam, sand, free draining
pH universal
H upright

Ocimum minimum
Bush Basil, French Basil

H1c *Lamiaceae family.* Clusters of small white
tubular flowers. Small green, oval, pointed,
aromatic leaves. Scatter whole leaves over
tomatoes, pasta & rice dishes.

annual
^30cm «20cm»
A full sun
S loam, sand,
free draining
pH universal
H upright

Ocimum minimum 'Greek'
Greek Basil

H1c *Lamiaceae family.* Clusters of small white
tubular flowers. Small green, oval, pointed,
aromatic leaves. Leaves can be rubbed on skin
to deter mosquitoes. Leaves & flowers are edible.

annual
^23cm «15cm»
A full sun
S loam, sand,
free draining
pH universal
H bushy

Ocimum tenuiflorum
Holy Basil, Purple Tulsi

H1c *Lamiaceae family.* Clusters of small pink/mauve
tubular flowers. Green/brown/purple, oval,
pointed, hairy & serrated leaves with a pungent
scent & flavour. Sacred herb of the Hindu.

annual
^30cm «20cm»
A full sun
S loam, sand,
free draining
pH universal
H upright

93

Olea europaea
Olea Tree

H4 *Oleaceae family.* Clusters of small cream flowers in summer, followed by green fruit that ripens to black .Oval, grey/green, leathery leaves with silver undersides. Green & black fruit are edible.

evergree tree
^up to 10m «up to 5m»
A full sun
S chalk, loam, sand,
  well drained
pH universal
H tree

Origanum dictamnus
Cretan Oregano

H4 *Lamiaceae family.* The tiny pink tubular flowers are surrounded by grey/green bracts that turn pink/purple with maturity. Highly aromatic, round, grey/green leaves. Leaves are edible.

evergreen sub-shrub
^15cm «40cm»
A full sun
S chalk, loam, sand,
  free draining
pH universal
H clump
! do not self-medicate

Origanum 'French'
French Marjoram

H4 *Lamiaceae family.* Clusters of tiny tubular pale pink flowers. Aromatic, oval, hairy leaves, which form a mat, are green in winter & gold in summer. Leaves have a light spicy flavour.

deciduous sub-shrub
^45cm «45cm»
A full sun, partial shade
S chalk, loam, sand,
  free draining
pH universal
H clump

Origanum 'Hot and Spicy'
Hot & Spicy Oregano

H4 *Lamiaceae family.* Clusters of white knotted
flowers Oval grey/green, slightly hairy leaves
that have a strong flavour. The spicy leaves go
with meat & vegetables.

deciduous sub-shrub
^60cm «45cm»
A full sun
S chalk, loam, sand,
   free draining
pH universal
H clump

Origanum 'Jekka's Beauty'
Jekka's Beauty Oregano

H4 *Lamiaceae family.* Tiny pretty pink flowers
surrounded by grey, green bracts that turn deep
pink/purple as they mature. Aromatic round,
slightly hairy, grey/green leaves. Edible flowers.

evergreen sub-shrub
^20cm «30cm»
A full sun
S chalk, loam, sand,
   free draining
pH universal
H clump

Origanum 'Kent Beauty'
Kent Beauty Oregano

H4 *Lamiaceae family.* Pretty pink flowers with grey/
green bracts that turn deep pink/purple as they
mature in summer. Aromatic, round, grey/green
leaves, with a pale green underside. Edible flowers.

evergreen sub-shrub
^20cm «30cm»
A full sun
S chalk, loam, sand,
   free draining
pH universal
H clump

Origanum majorana
Sweet Marjoram, Knotted Marjoram

H3

Lamiaceae family. Tiny white tubular flowers that grow around a green centre in a knot shape. Very aromatic, pale green, soft, oval leaves. Excellent flavour; use with meat, tomatoes & pasta.

perennial, often annual

^30cm «30cm»

A full sun

S chalk, loam, sand, free draining

pH universal

H clump

! do not self-medicate

Origanum majorana var. *tenuifolium*
Cypriot Marjoram

H2

Lamiaceae family. Tiny white tubular flowers that grow around a green centre in a knot shape. Small, aromatic, pale green, soft, oval leaves. Native of Cyprus. Lovely with Mediterranean food.

evergreen sub-shrub

^30cm «30cm»

A full sun

S chalk, loam, sand, free draining

pH universal

H clump

! do not self-medicate

Origanum x *majoricum*
Italian Marjoram

H3

Lamiaceae family. Tiny white tubular flowers covered in pale green bracts. Small, aromatic, pale green, soft, oval leaves. Native of Italy. Wonderful with tomato, pasta, pizza & breads.

evergreen sub-shrub

^45cm «45cm»

A full sun

S chalk, loam, sand, free draining

pH universal

H clump

! do not self-medicate

Origanum onites
Pot Marjoram

H4 *Lamiaceae family.* Clusters of tiny tubular mauve flowers. Dark green, aromatic, hairy leaves, which form a mat in winter. Use with meat & vegetable dishes.

deciduous sub-shrub
^45cm «45cm»
A full sun, partial shade
S chalk, loam, sand, free draining
pH universal
H clump
! do not self-medicate

Origanum 'Rosenkuppel'
Rosenkuppel Oregano

H4 *Lamiaceae family.* Clusters of very attractive, small, dark pink flowers . Dark green, oval, slightly hairy leaves. Flowers are edible.

deciduous sub-shrub
^60cm «45cm»
A full sun, partial shade
S chalk, loam, sand, free draining
pH universal
H clump

Origanum syriacum
Middle East Oregano, Za'attar

H4 *Lamiaceae family.* Clusters of white knotted flowers. Oval grey/green, slightly hairy leaves that have a strong flavour. Combine with sesame seeds & olive oil to make Za'attar.

evergreen sub-shrub
^60cm «45cm»
A full sun
S chalk, loam, sand, free draining
pH universal
H clump
! do not self-medicate

Origanum vulgare

Lamiaceae family. This group of oregano all have *vulgare* in their botanical name which literally translates as 'common'. Confusingly they are also often known as marjoram. They are a deciduous sub-shrub, height 20–45cm, spread 30–45cm with clusters of tiny tubular pale pink/mauve flowers. Aromatic, hairy leaves which form a mat in winter. The leaves in this group can vary from yellow or dark green to variegated cream & pale green. The flowers & leaves are edible, with a pungent, peppery flavour. Use with vegetable & meat dishes.

deciduous sub-shrub
^20–45cm «30–45cm»
A full sun, partial shade
S chalk, loam, sand, free draining
pH universal
H clump

Origanum vulgare
Oregano

H5 Mauve flowers. Vigour
& flavour can vary
depending on the
planting situation.
Dark green leaves.

! ^45cm «45cm»
! do not self-medicate

Origanum vulgare 'Acorn Bank'
Acorn Bank Oregano

H4 Pink flowers.
The golden yellow
leaves are prone to
sun scorch.

^45cm «45cm»

Origanum vulgare 'Aureum'
Golden Oregano

H4 Pink flowers with
golden leaves.

^45cm «45cm»

Origanum vulgare 'Compactum'
Compact Oregano

H4 Lovely large clusters
of small pink flowers.
Oval, green leaves.

^30cm «30cm»

Origanum vulgare 'Nanum'
Dwarf Oregano

H4 Small pale pink/white
flowers with oval,
green leaves.

^20cm «30cm»

Origanum vulgare 'Polyphant' (v)
Polyphant Oregano

H4 White flowers with
variegated white &
green leaves.

^30cm «30cm»

Papaver rhoeas
Field Poppy, Common Poppy

H3 *Papaveraceae family.* Large scarlet flowers with black stamens. Toothed & lobed green leaves. Seeds are used in baking.

annual
^up to 80cm «20cm»
A full sun
S chalk, loam, sand, free draining
pH universal
H upright

Perilla frutescens
Zi Su, Egoma

H2 *Lamiaceae family.* Small white/cream tubular flowers. Deeply cut green leaf with crinkled edges. Aromatic when crushed. Important Eastern culinary herb. Leaves & flowers are edible.

annual
^up to 1.2m «60cm»
A sun, partial shade
S chalk, loam, sand, free draining
pH universal
H upright
! can cause dermatitis

Perilla frutescens var. purpurascens
Purple Shiso

H2 *Lamiaceae family.* Small pink tubular flowers. Deeply cut dark purple leaf with crinkled bronzed edges. Important Japanese culinary herb. Leaves & flowers are edible, great in stir fries.

annual
^up to 1.2m «60cm»
A sun, partial shade
S chalk, loam, sand, free draining
pH universal
H upright
! can cause dermatitis

Persicaria hydropiper 'Rubra'
Red Water Pepper

H1c *Polygonaceae family.* Small pink flowers. Dark red, lance-shaped, aromatic foliage. Pungent highly flavoured leaves are used in Japanese & Vietnamese cooking; add just before serving.

perennial
^20–70cm «45cm»
A sun, partial shade
S damp loam, sand
pH universal
H upright

Persicaria odorata
Vietnamese Coriander, Rau Ram, Cambodian Mint

H2 *Polygonaceae family.* Small creamy white flowers, rarely produced under cultivation & in cold climates. Aromatic, pointed, green leaves with a brown V-shaped marking near the base.

evergreen perennial
^45cm «45cm»
A sun, partial shade
S damp loam, sand
pH universal
H upright

Petroselinum crispum
Parsley

H4 *Apiaceae family.* Small creamy white flowers in flat umbels in the summer of the 2nd year. Leaves are bright green, serrated, with variable curly toothed edges & a fresh mild flavour.

biennial
^up to 40cm «30cm»
A sun, partial shade
S damp fertile loam, sand
pH universal
H clump
! do not take if pregnant

P

Petroselinum crispum 'French'
French Parsley

H4 *Apiaceae family.* Small creamy white flowers in
flat umbels in summer of the 2nd season. Dark
green, divided leaves with serrated edges have a
strong flavour, & are rich in vitamins & minerals.

biennial
^up to 60cm «30cm»
A sun, partial shade
S damp fertile loam, sand
pH universal
H clump
! do not take if pregnant

Plectranthus amboinicus
Cuban Oregano

H1c *Lamiaceae family.* Small, tubular pale lilac
flowers. Large, succulent, pale green leaves.
Good with chicken, fish & risotto. Used to make
Creole Chicken in the West Indies.

evergreen perennial
^up to 80cm «up to
60cm»
A full sun
S light loam, sand,
free draining
pH neutral
H clump

Porophyllum ruderale
Quilquina, Bolivian Coriander

H1c *Asteraceae family.* Cluster of tiny yellow flowers
which develop into a dandelion clock. The
fragrant leaves are used in South American
cooking. Use fresh leaves in salads & salsas.

annual
^up to 80cm «20cm»
A full sun
S light loam, sand,
free draining
pH neutral
H clump

Portulaca oleracea
Purslane

H2   *Portulacaceae family.* Small yellow, stalkless 4–6-petalled flowers which open in the sun & close in the shade. Thick fleshy mid-green leaves. A popular salad herb, high in Omega 3.

- annual
- ^45cm «60cm»
- **A** sun, partial shade
- **S** light loam, sand, free draining
- **pH** universal
- **H** clump

Primula veris
Cowslip

H5   *Primulaceae family.* Yellow drooping flowers are grouped together, with up to 30 flowers per head. Sweetly scented. Mid-green, oval, textured, finely haired leaves. Edible flowers.

- herbaceous perennial
- ^20cm «20cm»
- **A** sun, partial shade
- **S** clay, loam, sand
- **pH** universal
- **H** clump
- **!** do not take if pregnant

Primula vulgaris
Primrose

H5   *Primulaceae family.* Sweetly scented, single, pale yellow with dark yellow centre flower. Finely haired stems. Mid-green, oval, textured leaves. Edible flowers.

- herbaceous perennial
- ^15cm «15cm»
- **A** sun, partial shade
- **S** clay, loam, sand
- **pH** universal
- **H** clump
- **!** do not take if pregnant

Prostanthera rotundifolia
Australian Mint Bush

H2 *Lamiaceae family.* Very attractive purple
bell-shaped flowers. Small, oval, peppermint-
scented, grey/green leaves. A traditional
medicinal herb of Australia.

evergreen shrub
^up to 2m «60cm»
A full sun
S chalk, loam, sand,
   well-drained
pH universal
H bushy

Punica granatum
Pomegranate, Carthaginian Apple

H3 *Lythraceae family.* Lovely red flower followed
by leathery red fruits. Green, glossy, narrow
oblong leaves. New growth is bronze-coloured.
Fruit is used in sweet & savoury dishes.

deciduous shrub
^up to 2.5m «up to 2.5m»
A full sun
S loam, sand, free draining
pH acid–neutral
H bushy

Pycnanthemum pilosum
Mountain Mint

H5 *Lamiaceae family.* Small white/pale lavender
tubular flowers with purple spots on lower lip.
Oblong, lance-shaped pointed grey/green hairy
leaves. Use leaves for marinades & teas.

herbaceous perennial
^60cm «60cm»
A sun, partial shade
S clay, loam, sand, free
   draining
pH universal
H upright

Rosmarinus officinalis See page 106–111

Rumex acetosa
Sorrel, Broad Leaved Sorrel

H5 *Polygonaceae family.* Inconspicuous green flowers that turn brown as seeds ripen. Mid-green, lance-shaped leaves, with a strong lemon flavour. Leaves can be eaten fresh or cooked.

herbaceous perennial
^up to 45cm «60cm»
A sun, partial shade
S chalk, loam, fertile
  sand, free draining
pH acid–neutral
H clump

Rumex sanguineus var. *sanguines*
Red Veined Sorrel, Bloody Dock

H5 *Polygonaceae family.* Inconspicuous green flowers that turn brown as seeds ripen. The mid-green, lanced-shaped leaves have a striking red veins & an acid taste. Eat young leaves when fresh.

herbaceous perennial
^up to 45cm
  «up to 45cm»
A sun, partial shade
S chalk, loam, fertile
  sand, free draining
pH acid–neutral
H clump

Rumex scutatus
Buckler Leaf Sorrel, French Sorrel

H5 *Polygonaceae family.* Inconspicuous green flowers that turn brown as seeds ripen. Mid-green, squat shield-shaped leaves, which taste like granny smith apples. Leaves are edible.

herbaceous perennial
^up to 45cm
  «up to 60cm»
A sun, partial shade
S chalk, loam, fertile
  sand, free draining
pH acid–neutral
H clump

Rosmarinus – Prostrate

Lamiaceae family. Prostrate Rosemaries grow flatter than the arching form. They are ideal in well-drained soil as ground cover or for an edging onto gravel. They are also suitable for containers or for growing over a wall. Evergreen shrub, height 10 –40cm, spread 50cm–90cm. Small flowers vary in colour from white & pink to pale or dark blue. Short needle-shaped, dark to mid-green, highly aromatic leaves. Both flowers & leaves can be used, good with vegetables, tomatoes, meat, fish & pasta dishes.

evergreen shrub
^10–40cm «50cm–90cm»
A full sun
S chalk, clay, loam, sand, free draining
pH universal
H prostrate
! do not ingest essential oil or use the leaf in excess

Rosmarinus officinalis 'Fota Blue'
Rosemary Fota Blue

H4   Striking small, dark blue flowers.

^40cm «60cm»

Rosmarinus officinalis 'Haifa'
Rosemary Haifa

H3   Pale blue flowers. Good for containers.

^10cm «50cm»

Rosmarinus officinalis (Prostratus Group)
Rosemary Prostrate

H4 Small pale
blue flowers.

^30cm «60cm»

Rosmarinus officinalis (Prostratus Group) 'Capri'
Rosemary Capri

H3 Small pale
blue flowers.

^15cm «60cm»

Rosmarinus officinalis (Prostratus Group) '**Whitewater Silver**' Rosemary Whitewater Silver

H3 Pale blue flowers.
Silver underside
to leaves.

^15cm «60cm»

Rosmarinus officinalis 'Severn Sea'
Rosemary Severn Sea

H4 Blue flowers. Good for
hanging down walls.

^40cm «90cm»

Rosmarinus – Upright

Lamiaceae family. This form of Rosemary is ideal to be grown as a specimen or as a hedge. It is an evergreen shrub, height & spread 80cm–1m, with small flowers that can vary in colour from white & pink to pale or dark blue. Short needle-shaped, dark to mid-green, highly aromatic leaves. It can be used throughout the year. Both the flowers & leaves are edible, good with vegetables, tomatoes, meat, fish & pasta dishes. A small sprig of leaves can be also used to make a lovely reviving tisane.

evergreen shrub
^80cm–1m «80cm–1m»
A full sun
S chalk, clay, loam, sand,
   free draining
pH universal
H upright
! do not ingest essential oil
   or use the leaf in excess

Rosmarinus officinalis
Rosemary

H5   Small pale
 blue flowers.

   ^up to 1m «up to 1m»

Rosmarinus officinalis 'Green Ginger'
Rosemary Green Ginger

H4   Small blue flowers.
     Ginger-scented
     leaves.

   ^90cm «90cm»

Rosmarinus officinalis 'Miss Jessopp's Upright'
Rosemary Miss Jessopp's Upright

H5   Small pale
blue flowers.

^up to 1m «up to 1m»

Rosmarinus officinalis 'Roseus'
Rosemary Pink

H5   Small pale
pink flowers.

^80cm «80cm»

Rosmarinus officinalis 'Sissinghurst Blue'
Rosemary Sissinghurst Blue

H5   Small dark
blue flowers.

^80cm «80cm»

Rosmarinus officinalis 'Sudbury Blue'
Rosemary Sudbury Blue

H5   Small pale
blue flowers.

^up to 1m «up to 1m»

Rosmarinus – Upright Arching

H4 *Lamiaceae family.* Arching Rosemaries have the most attractive habit as they are both upright & trailing with beautiful arching branches. They can be grown so they hang over a wall or in a container where they look beautiful. Evergreen shrub, height 40–90cm, spread 60cm –90cm. Small flowers vary in colour from white & pink to pale or dark blue. Short needle-shaped, dark to mid-green, highly aromatic leaves. It can be used throughout the year. Flowers & leaves are edible, good with vegetables, tomatoes, meat, fish & pasta dishes, or use leaves to make a tisane.

evergreen shrub
^40–90cm «60cm–90cm»
A full sun
S chalk, clay, loam, sand, free draining
pH universal
H upright, arching
! do not ingest essential oil or use the leaf in excess

Rosmarinus officinalis f. albiflorus 'Lady in White'   Rosemary Lady in White

Small exquisite white flowers.

^60cm «60cm»

Rosmarinus officinalis 'Foxtail'
Rosemary Foxtail

Small pale blue flowers, leaves have a light silver underside.

^60cm «60cm»

Rosmarinus officinalis 'Jekka's Blue'
Rosemary Jekka's Blue

Small dark
blue flowers.

^70cm «70cm»

Rosmarinus officinalis 'Majorca Pink'
Rosemary Majorca Pink

Pale pink flowers with
dark line in lower lip.

^90cm «90cm»

Rosmarinus officinalis (Prostratus Group) 'Rampant Boule'   Rosemary Rampant Boule

Small blue flowers.
Leaves have a light
silver underside.

^40cm «60cm»

Rosmarinus officinalis 'Vatican Blue'
Rosemary Vatican Blue

Small bright
blue flowers.

^70cm «70cm»

Rungia klossii
Mushroom Plant

H1c

Acanthaceae family. Showy blue flower, rarely flowers in cold climates. Thick glossy dark green leaves. Higher in protein than mushrooms, it contains many vitamins & minerals. Edible leaves.

evergreen perennial
^60cm «45cm»
A partial shade
S fertile loam
pH acid–neutral
H upright

Ruta graveolens
Rue

H5

Rutaceae family. Small, yellow waxy flowers with 4 or 5 petals. Green/blue leaves are prettily divided into small rounded oval lobes & have an odd scent. Leaves have a very bitter taste, use with caution.

evergreen shrub
^60cm «60cm»
A sun, partial shade
S loam, sand,
  free draining
pH universal
H upright
! can cause minor burns

Ruta graveolens 'Alderley Blue'
Alderley Blue Rue

H5

Rutaceae family. Small, yellow, waxy flowers with 4–5 petals. Blue leaves are very prettily divided into small rounded oval lobes & have an odd scent. Leaves have a very bitter taste, use with caution.

evergreen shrub
^40cm «60cm»
A sun, partial shade
S loam, sand,
  free draining
pH universal
H upright
! can cause minor burns

Salvia argentea
Silver Sage

H4 *Lamiaceae family.* White, with a hint of pink, flowers in 2nd season. Splendid large silvery grey leaves covered in long silvery white hairs. Flowers are edible.

biennial
^60cm «30cm»
A full sun
S chalk, loam, sand, free draining
pH universal
H upright

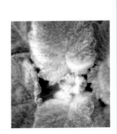

Salvia elegans 'Scarlet Pineapple'
Pineapple Sage

H3 *Lamiaceae family.* Long thin trumpet-shaped red flowers. Oval, pointed, green leaves with a slight red/brown tinge to the edges & a pineapple scent when crushed. Flowers & leaves are edible.

herbaceous shrub
^90cm «60cm»
A full sun
S chalk, loam, sand, free draining
pH universal
H bushy

Salvia elegans 'Tangerine'
Tangerine Scented Sage

H3 *Lamiaceae family.* Long thin trumpet-shaped red flowers. Oval, pointed, green, ribbed leaves with a slight red/brown tinge to the edges & a tangerine scent when crushed. Flowers & leaves are edible.

herbaceous shrub
^up to 75cm «60cm»
A full sun
S chalk, loam, sand, free draining
pH universal
H bushy

Salvia lavandulifolia
Narrow Leaved Sage

H4 *Lamiaceae family.* Attractive blue flowers. Small, narrow, oval, textured, highly aromatic leaves with an excellent sage flavour. Flowers & leaves are edible, good with rice & chicken.

evergreen shrub
^60cm «60cm»
A full sun
S chalk, loam, sand, free draining
pH universal
H clump
! do not over-use

Salvia lavandulifolia 'Nazareth'
Israeli Sage

H4 *Lamiaceae family.* Pretty blue flowers. Small, narrow, oval grey leaves covered in fine silver hairs. Flowers & leaves are edible, good with rice & chicken dishes.

evergreen shrub
^60cm «60cm»
A full sun
S chalk, loam, sand, free draining
pH universal
H clump
! do not over-use

Salvia microphylla var. *microphylla*
Blackcurrant Sage

H4 *Lamiaceae family.* Lovely raspberry-coloured flowers with the distinctive lower lip, Oval, mid-green, aromatic leaves which smell of blackcurrant but taste awful. Flowers are edible.

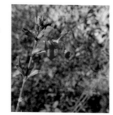

evergreen shrub
^up to 1.2m «up to 1.2m»
A full sun
S chalk, loam, sand, free draining
pH universal
H bushy

Salvia officinalis
Sage, Common Sage

H4 *Lamiaceae family.* Mauve/blue flowers. Highly
aromatic, finely veined, oval, greeny/grey,
textured leaves. Flowers & leaves are edible. Use
leaves with rice, vegetables & meat dishes.

evergreen shrub
^75cm «75cm»
A full sun
S chalk, loam, sand,
free draining
pH universal
H bushy
! do not over-use

Salvia officinalis 'Albiflora'
White Flowering Sage

H4 *Lamiaceae family.* White flowers. Highly
aromatic, finely veined, oval, green/grey,
textured leaves. Flowers & leaves are edible. Use
leaves with rice, vegetables & meat dishes.

evergreen shrub
^75cm «75cm»
A full sun
S chalk, loam, sand,
free draining
pH universal
H bushy
! do not over-use

Salvia officinalis 'Berggarten'
Berggarten Sage

H5 *Lamiaceae family.* The occasional pale violet
flower. Highly aromatic, finely veined, oval,
grey, textured leaves. Flowers & leaves are
edible. Use leaves with rice, vegetables & meat.

evergreen shrub
^60cm «60cm»
A full sun
S chalk, loam, sand,
free draining
pH universal
H bushy
! do not over-use

Salvia officinalis broad-leaved
Broad Leaved Sage

H5

Lamiaceae family. Non-flowering. Highly aromatic, finely veined, oval, grey textured leaves. Bushy spreading habit. Use leaves with rice, vegetables & meat dishes.

evergreen shrub
^60cm «60cm»
A full sun
S chalk, loam, sand,
   free draining
pH universal
H bushy
! do not over-use

Salvia officinalis 'Greek'
Greek Sage

H4

Lamiaceae family. Mauve/blue flowers. Highly aromatic, finely veined, oval, grey/green, textured leaves with an extra lobe near the stem. Flowers & leaves are edible.

evergreen shrub
^90cm «90cm»
A full sun
S chalk, loam, sand,
   free draining
pH universal
H bushy
! do not over-use

Salvia officinalis 'Icterina' (v)
Gold Sage

H5
Lamiaceae family. Light blue flowers. Highly aromatic, finely veined, variegated gold, green & grey, textured leaves. Bushy spreading habit. Flowers & leaves are edible.

evergreen shrub
^60cm «60cm»
A full sun
S chalk, loam, sand,
   free draining
pH universal
H bushy
! do not over-use

Salvia officinalis 'Purpurascens'
Purple Sage

H5 *Lamiaceae family.* Purple/blue flowers. Highly
 aromatic, finely veined, oval, purple textured
leaves that turn grey/green when mature. Bushy
spreading habit. Flowers & leaves are edible.

evergreen shrub
^85cm «85cm»
A full sun
S chalk, loam, sand,
   free draining
pH universal
H bushy
! do not over-use

Salvia officinalis 'Roseus'
Pink Flowering Sage

H4 *Lamiaceae family.* Pink flowers. Highly aromatic,
finely veined, oval, grey textured leaves. Bushy
spreading habit. Flowers & leaves are edible. Use
leaves with rice, vegetables & meat dishes.

evergreen shrub
^60cm «60cm»
A full sun
S chalk, loam, sand,
   free draining
pH universal
H bushy
! do not over-use

Salvia officinalis 'Tricolor' (v)
Tricolour Sage

H3 *Lamiaceae family.* Pale blue flowers. Highly
aromatic, finely veined, oval, grey/green leaves
that are variegated with cream & splashes of
purple. Flowers & leaves are edible.

evergreen shrub
^50cm «50cm»
A full sun
S chalk, loam, sand,
   free draining
pH universal
H bushy
! do not over-use

Salvia sclarea
Clary Sage

H4 *Lamiaceae family.* Long racemes of pale pink flowers with mauve/pink bracts. Strongly scented, wrinkled, oblong, grey/green leaves. Flowers are edible, & look good in salads & ice cubes.

 biennial
^60cm «60cm»
A full sun
S chalk, loam, sand, free draining
pH universal
H upright

Salvia viridis
Painted Sage, Red Topped Sage

H3 *Lamiaceae family.* Small purple & white or pink flowers, & colourful sterile bracts of purple, pink, blue & white, often with green veins & green, aromatic leaves. Flowers & bracts are edible.

 annual
^45cm «20cm»
A full sun
S chalk, loam, sand, free draining
pH universal
H upright

Sanguisorba minor
Salad Burnet, Pimpernel

H5 *Rosaceae family.* Tiny magenta flowers in compact heads on stalks that stand a foot or so above the leaves. Soft grey/green leaves are divided into neat ovals with toothed edges.

 evergreen perennial
^up to 60cm «30cm»
A full sun
S chalk, loam, sand, free draining
pH neutral–alkaline
H clump

Santolina corsica Jord. & Fourr.
Corsican Santolina

H4 *Asteraceae family.* Yellow button flowers. Aromatic, silver, narrow leaves divided into serrated small linear segments. When dried, the leaves are a very good moth repellent.

evergreen shrub
^75cm «75cm»
A full sun
S chalk, loam, sand, free draining
pH universal
H bushy

Satureja biflora
Lemon Savory, African Savory

H3 *Lamiaceae family.* Small white/pink lemon-flavoured flowers. Narrow, green, lemon-scented leaves. Both flower & leaf have a lemon flavour, great with fish, meat & vegetable dishes.

evergreen shrub
^30cm «30cm»
A full sun
S loam, free draining
pH neutral–alkaline
H clump
! do not take if pregnant

Satureja douglasii
Yerba Buena

H3 *Lamiaceae family.* Tiny white flowers. Small, mid-green, mint-scented leaves. In the right climate this makes great ground cover. The mint leaves are good in drinks & with vegetables.

evergreen perennial
^4cm «up to 2m»
A full sun
S loam, free draining
pH neutral–alkaline
H clump
! do not take if pregnant

Satureja hortensis
Summary Savory, St Julian's Herb

H2   *Lamiaceae family.* Small whorled white flowers. Narrow, small, lance-shaped, aromatic, green/brown leaves. Known as the bean herb as the leaves are cooked with all forms of beans & pulses.

annual
^25cm «25cm»
A full sun
S loam, sand,
   free draining
pH neutral–alkaline
H upright
! do not take if pregnant

Satureja montana
Winter Savory

H4   *Lamiaceae family.* Small white, tinged with pink, flowers. Dark green, linear, pungent, aromatic leaves. Good for salt-free diets, add the leaves to bean dishes, stews & soups.

partial evergreen shrub
^45cm «45cm»
A full sun
S loam, free draining
pH neutral–alkaline
H clump
! do not take if pregnant

Satureja montana subsp. *Illyrica*
Illyrica Savory

H4   *Lamiaceae family.* Attractive small purple flowers. Dark green, linear, pungent, aromatic leaves. Flowers & leaves are edible, good for salt-free diets & with beans, stews & soups.

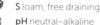

partial evergreen shrub
^30cm «30cm»
A full sun
S loam, free draining
pH neutral–alkaline
H clump
! do not take if pregnant

Satureja spicigera
Creeping Savory

H4 *Lamiaceae family.* Tiny white flowers in late summer. Bright green, linear, highly pungent leaves. The native Savory of Sardinia. Leaves & flowers are edible, good for salt-free diets.

herbaceous perennial
^8cm «75cm»
A full sun
S loam, sand, free draining
pH neutral–alkaline
H mat forming, creeping
! do not take if pregnant

Sempervivum tectorum
House Leek

H5 *Crassulaceae family.* Pink star-shaped flowers, can take many years to flower. Grey/green, succulent, oval leaves with darker points. Broken/crushed leaves can be applied to nettle rash.

evergreen succulent
^up to 15cm «20cm»
A full sun
S loam, sand, free draining
pH universal
H clump

Stevia rebaudiana
Stevia, Kaa-he-e, Aztec Herb

H3 *Asteraceae family.* Small white flowers in late summer. Lance-shaped, bright green leaves. Native to Paraguay & Brazil. Leaves are sweet tasting & can be used as a sugar substitute.

herbaceous perennial
^up to 60cm «45cm»
A sun, partial shade
S moist loam, sand
pH slightly acid–neutral
H clump
! leaf banned for culinary use in EU

Symphytum officinale
Comfrey

H7   *Boraginaceae family.* Clusters of white, purple
or pink tubular flowers. Green, lance-shaped,
hairy leaves. Medicinal; roots & leaves. Leaves
can be used to make a liquid feed.

herbaceous perennial
^up to 1m «up to 1m»
A sun, partial shade
S chalk, clay, loam, sand
pH universal
H upright
! do not self-medicate

Symphytum x uplandicum
Russian Comfrey

H7   *Boraginaceae family.* Clusters of purple or pink
tubular flowers. Green, lance-shaped, hairy
leaves. Medicinal; roots & leaves. Leaves can be
used to make a liquid feed.

herbaceous perennial
^up to 1m «up to 1m»
A sun, partial shade
S chalk, clay, loam, sand
pH universal
H upright
! do not self-medicate

Tagetes lucida
Winter Tarragon, Sweet Mace

H3   *Asteraceae family.* Small clusters of golden
flowers. Narrow, lance-shaped, toothed leaves,
strong aniseed flavour. In cool climates, this dies
back in early spring, reappearing in early summer.

herbaceous perennial
^up to 80cm «45cm»
A full sun
S light loam
pH slightly acid–neutral
H bushy

Tanacetum balsamita
Alecost, Costmary

H5 *Asteraceae family.* Clusters of small daisy-like white flowers. Large rosettes of oval, aromatic, soft, silver/grey/green leaves. Rub a fresh leaf on stings or bites to relieve pain. Used to make ale.

herbaceous perennial
^up to 1m «45cm»
A full sun
S loam, sand,
   free draining
pH universal
H upright

Tanacetum parthenium
Feverfew

H6 *Asteraceae family.* Clusters of small white, daisy-like flowers. Mid-green, lobed & divided leaves with lightly serrated edges. Young leaves have a bitter flavour; use in salads or with cheese.

herbaceous perennial
^up to 1.2m «45cm»
A full sun
S loam, sand, free draining
pH universal
H clump
! wear gloves to handle

Tanacetum vulgare
Tansy

H6 *Asteraceae family.* Clusters of yellow button-like flowers. Aromatic, dark green, feathery, divided leaves with toothed edges. Dried bunches of tansy flowers & leaves make a good fly repellent.

herbaceous perennial
^up to 1.2m «indefinite»
A full sun
S loam, sand, free draining
pH universal
H upright
! wear gloves to handle

Teucrium x lucidrys
Hedge Germander

H6 *Lamiaceae family.* Small pink flowers. Aromatic, dark green, oval, lightly toothed leaves with a shiny surface & a matt underside. In Elizabethan times this was the traditional edging plant.

evergreen perennial
^45cm «30cm»
A full sun
S chalk, loam, sand, free draining
pH neutral–alkaline
H clump

Teucrium marum
Cat Thyme

H4 *Lamiaceae family.* Small pink flowers. Very aromatic, small grey leaves, similar to thyme. Native Spanish herb. Cats adore this plant, it makes them blissful.

evergreen shrub
^30cm «45cm»
A full sun
S chalk, loam, sand, free draining
pH neutral–alkaline
H clump

Teucrium scorodonia
Wood Sage

H6 *Lamiaceae family.* Pale greenish-white flowers in summer. Soft, green, heart-shaped leaves with finely toothed edges. The bitter tasting leaves can be used to flavour ales & beers.

herbaceous perennial
^60cm «30cm»
A sun, partial shade
S chalk, loam, sand, free draining
pH neutral–alkaline
H clump
! do not self-medicate

Thymus herba-barona
Caraway Scented Thyme

H4 *Lamiaceae family.* Terminal clusters of small rose pink flowers. Oval, dark green, caraway-scented leaves. Edible flowers & leaves have a caraway flavour, good with cheese, egg & chicken dishes.

evergreen shrub
^3cm «60cm»
A full sun
S chalk, loam, sand, free draining
pH universal
H mat forming, creeping

Thymus herba-barona 'Lemon-scented'
Lemon Caraway Scented Thyme

H4 *Lamiaceae family.* Terminal clusters of small pale pink flowers. Small, oval, light green, lemon-scented leaves. Edible flowers & leaves have a lemon flavour, good with fish & chicken.

evergreen shrub
^3cm «60cm»
A full sun
S chalk, loam, sand, free draining
pH universal
H mat forming, creeping

Thymus mat forming, mound forming & upright *See page 126 –131*

Thymus polytrichus 'A. Kern. ex Borbás' subsp. *britannicus* (Ronniger) 'Kerguélen'
Wooly Thyme

H4 *Lamiaceae family.* Terminal clusters of small pale pink flowers. Small, oval, pale green, hairy aromatic leaves. Edible flowers & leaves.

evergreen shrub
^3cm «80cm»
A full sun
S chalk, loam, sand, free draining
pH universal
H mat forming, creeping

Thymus – Mat Forming

H4 *Lamiaceae family.* Mat forming creeping thymes are a lovely group; they are ideal for growing in gravel or for growing as a thyme walk in very well-drained soil. They are an evergreen shrub, height 2–3cm, spread 40cm. Terminal clusters of small, white, pink, mauve, purple or red flowers. Aromatic, small sometimes tiny, oval grey/green leaves which are often covered in fine white hairs. Flowers & leaves are edible, however the leaves are often too small to harvest. Use flowers in salads both sweet & savory.

evergreen shrub
^2–3cm «45cm»
A full sun
S chalk, loam, sand, free draining
pH universal
H mat forming, creeping

Thymus 'Carbon Wine and Roses'
Carbon Wine and Roses Thyme

Terminal clusters of small purple/pink flowers with a dark crimson splash. Dark green leaves.

^3cm «45cm»

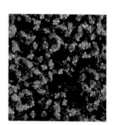

Thymus Coccineus Group
Creeping Red Thyme

Terminal clusters of small stunning magenta flowers. Dark green leaves.

^3cm «45cm»

Thymus 'Dartmoor'
Dartmoor Thyme

Terminal clusters of purple/pink flowers.

^3cm «45cm»

Thymus 'Hartington Silver'
Hartington Silver Thyme

Terminal clusters of small pale pink flowers. Variegated pale green, white & silver leaves.

^3cm «45cm»

Thymus 'Jekka's Rosy Carpet'
Jekka's Rosy Carpet Thyme

Terminal clusters of small pink flowers with a dark purple splash. Dark green leaves.

^3cm «45cm»

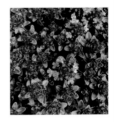

Thymus 'Pink Ripple'
Pink Ripple Thyme

Terminal clusters of small shell pink flowers. Olive green leaves, with a pale underside.

^3cm «45cm»

Thymus – Mound Forming

H4 *Lamiaceae family.* Mound forming thymes grow in a neat low mound; they look lovely combined with matt forming thymes in a thyme walk, or as garden edging. They also look most attractive in containers. Evergreen shrub, height 4–15cm, spread 30–60cm. Terminal clusters of small flowers that can vary in colour from white, pink & mauve to purple & red. Highly aromatic, small sometimes tiny, oval grey to bright green leaves. Flowers & leaves are edible, however some leaves are too small to harvest. Use flowers in salads, both sweet & savory.

evergreen shrub
^4–15cm «30–60cm»
A full sun
S chalk, loam, sand, free draining
pH universal
H mound forming, creeping

Thymus caespititius
Cretan Thyme

Pink flowers. Narrow bright green, pine resin-scented leaves.

^8cm «45cm»
! do not take
   if pregnant

Thymus camphoratus
Camphor Thyme

Pink flowers with bracts in summer. Succulent, camphor-scented leaves.

^15cm «30cm»
! do not take if pregnant

Thymus 'Doone Valley'
Doone Valley Thyme

Pink/purple flowers.
Small, lemon-
scented, bright
green, variegated
with gold leaves.

^4cm «45cm»

Thymus 'Iden'
Iden Thyme

Pale pink flowers.
Mid-green aromatic
edible leaves.

^10cm «60cm»

Thymus 'Jekka'
Jekka's Thyme

Pink flowers with
a dark purple line on
lower lip. Bright green
leaves with a good
culinary flavour.

^10cm «60cm»

Thymus 'Pinewood'
Pinewood Thyme

Pale pink flowers.
Pine-scented green
leaves.

^15cm «45cm»
! do not take
if pregnant

Thymus – Upright

H4

Lamiaceae family. There are many forms of upright thymes; they are taller & more open growing than the mound forms. They make a good edge to a herb garden & also grow well in groups or in containers. Evergreen shrub, height 25–30cm, spread 25–45cm. Terminal clusters of small flowers that vary in colour from white & pink to mauve & purple. Highly aromatic, small oval grey/green leaves. These thymes are all excellent in the kitchen. Flowers & leaves are edible, & can be used with fish, chicken, vegetable & pasta dishes & many puddings.

evergreen shrub
^25–30cm «25–45cm»
A full sun
S chalk, loam, sand, free draining
pH universal
H upright

Thymus 'Culinary Lemon'
Lemon Thyme

Mauve flowers with dark green, lemon-scented leaves.

^30cm «30cm»

Thymus 'Fragrantissimus'
Orange Scented Thyme

Pale pink, bordering on white flowers. Grey/green leaves with spicy flavour.

^30cm «45cm»

Thymus 'Golden Lemon'
Golden Lemon Thyme

Purple/pink flowers
with lemon-scented
variegated dark green
& gold leaves.

^30cm «30cm»

Thymus 'Porlock'
Porlock Thyme

Magenta pink
flowers with dark
green leaves.

^30cm «30cm»

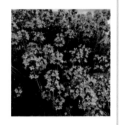

Thymus 'Silver Posie'
Silver Posie Thyme

Mauve flowers. Small
variegated silver, white
& green leaves with a
hint of pink on the tips.

^30cm «30cm»

Thymus 'Silver Queen'
Silver Queen Thyme

Mauve flowers.
Lemon-scented,
variegated silver, white
& green leaves.

^30cm «30cm»

Thymus pulegioides – Broad Leaved

H4 *Lamiaceae family.* Broad-leaved thymes have large leaves which makes them easy to pick for use in the kitchen. Some have a loose mounding habit & others creeping habits which are ideal for containers or for use in the garden as ground cover. Evergreen shrub, height 6–20cm, spread 40–60cm. Terminal clusters of small pink/purple flowers. Small dark green to gold oval leaves. Flowers & leaves are edible, & can be used with fish, chicken, vegetable & pasta dishes. They are also good with many puddings & in baking.

evergreen shrub
^6–20cm «40–60cm»
A full sun
S chalk, loam, sand, free draining
pH universal
H mound, forming creeping

Thymus pulegioides
Broad Leaved Thyme

Pink/purple flowers.

^20cm «60cm»
! do not take
if pregnant

Thymus pulegioides 'Archers Gold'
Archers Gold Thyme

Pink/purple flowers.

^20cm «60cm»

Thymus pulegioides 'Aureus'
Golden Thyme

  Pink/purple flowers.

^15cm «60cm»

Thymus pulegioides 'Bertram Anderson'
Bertram Anderson Thyme

Pink/purple flowers.

^20cm «40cm»

Thymus pulegioides 'Foxley' (v)
Foxley Thyme

Pink/purple flowers
with variegated dark
green/cream/white
leaves.

^20cm «60cm»

Thymus pulegioides 'Kurt'
Creeping Lemon Thyme

 Pink/purple flowers
with lemon-scented
leaves.

^6cm «60cm»

Thymus serpyllum – Creeping

H4 *Lamiaceae family.* These creeping thymes grow even lower than the mat forming thymes. Plant in well-drained soil, in gravel or on a sunny bank. Evergreen shrub, height 2–3cm, spread 45–80cm. Terminal clusters of small flowers that can vary in colour from white & pink to mauve & purple. Oval dark green to mid-green, sometime variegated with yellow &/or cream, small, hairy, aromatic leaves. Flowers & leaves are edible; however the leaves are often too small to harvest. Use flowers in salads, both sweet & savory.

evergreen shrub
^2–3cm «45–80cm»
A full sun
S chalk, loam, sand, free draining
pH universal
H mat forming, creeping

Thymus serpyllum
Creeping Thyme

White, pink, mauve or purple flowers. Dark green leaves.

^3cm «80cm»

Thymus serpyllum 'Annie Hall'
Annie Hall Thyme

Pale pink flowers. Pale green leaves.

^3cm «80cm»

Thymus serpyllum 'Goldstream'
Goldstream Thyme

Pale mauve flowers.
Variegated green,
yellow & cream leaves.

^3cm «80cm»

Thymus serpyllum 'Magic Carpet'
Magic Carpet Thyme

Terminal clusters
of small white/pink/
mauve flowers with
dark green leaves.

^3cm «80cm»

Thymus serpyllum 'Russetings'
Russetings Thyme

Purple flowers.
Dark green leaves.

^3cm «80cm»

Thymus serpyllum 'Snowdrift'
Snowdrift Thyme

White flowers.
Mid-green leaves.

^3cm «80cm»

Thymus vulgaris – Common Thyme

H4 *Lamiaceae family.* This group of thymes all have the Latin *vulgaris*, meaning common, in their name. They have an upright bushy habit, great as an edging plant or growing in containers. This form of thyme has the best culinary flavour & different forms can be found throughout the world. Evergreen shrub, height 30cm & spread 30–45cm. Terminal clusters of small pale mauve /pink/white flowers. Oval, narrow, pointed, dark to mid-green, small aromatic leaves. Edible flowers & leaves. Use with sauces, marinades, stuffings, stews, vegetables & pasta.

evergreen shrub
^30cm «30–45cm»
A full sun
S chalk, loam, sand, free draining
pH universal
H upright
! Do not take if pregnant

Thymus vulgaris
Common Thyme, Garden Thyme

Pale mauve flowers.
Dark green leaves.

^30cm «30cm»

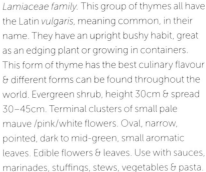

Thymus vulgaris 'Compactus'
Compact Thyme

Pale pink flowers with dark green leaves.

^30cm «30cm»

Thymus vulgaris 'French'
French Thyme

Very pale pink flowers. Grey/green aromatic leaves.

^30cm «30cm»

Thymus vulgaris 'Italian'
Italian Thyme

Very pale pink flowers with grey/green leaves.

^30cm «30cm»

Thymus vulgaris 'Snow White'
Compact White Thyme

White flowers with bright green aromatic leaves.

^30cm «30cm»

Tropaeolum majus 'Empress of India'
Nasturtium Empress of India

H2 *Tropaeolaceae family.* Dark red helmet-shaped flowers with a long nectar spur. Round, mid-green leaves that have a peppery flavour. Flowers & leaves are edible. Use in salads.

annual
^20cm «30cm»
A sun, partial shade
S light loam,
free draining
pH neutral
H bushy

Tulbaghia violacea
Society Garlic

H3 *Alliaceae family.* Fragrant, pale purple, star-shaped flowers in large terminal umbels. Grey/green, onion-scented, long narrow leaves. Native of South Africa. Edible flowers.

evergreen perennial
^50cm «20cm»
A full sun
S loam, sand,
free draining
pH universal
H clump

Tulbaghia violacea 'Silver Lace'
Society Garlic Silver Lace

H3 *Alliaceae family.* Fragrant, pale purple, star-shaped flowers in large terminal umbels. Variegated grey/green/cream, onion-scented & flavoured, long narrow leaves. Edible flowers.

evergreen perennial
^50cm «20cm»
A full sun
S loam, sand,
free draining
pH universal
H clump

Ugni molinae
Chilean Guava

H4 *Myrtaceae family.* Pale pink flowers, then round fruit which ripen to dark red. Small, oval, aromatic, dark green, leathery leaves, which in autumn can have copper tinges. Use fruit for jams & salads.

evergreen shrub
^up to 2.5m «1.5m»
A sun, partial shade
S chalk, clay, loam,
   sand, free draining
pH universal
H bushy

Ugni molinae 'Orange'
Orange Chilean Guava

H4 *Myrtaceae family.* Pretty pale pink flowers, then round fruit which ripen to very dark red. Small, oval, aromatic, dark green, leathery leaves with profound orange tips. Use fruit to make jam.

evergreen shrub
^up to 2.5m «1.5m»
A sun, partial shade
S chalk, clay, loam,
   sand, free draining
pH universal
H bushy

Ugni molinae 'Variegata' (v)
Variegated Chilean Guava

H4 *Myrtaceae family.* Pale pink flowers, then round fruit which ripen to very dark red. Small, oval, aromatic, variegated green/cream/yellow, leathery leaves. Use fruit for jams & salads.

evergreen shrub
^up to 2.5m «1.5m»
A sun, partial shade
S chalk, clay, loam,
   sand, free draining
pH universal
H bushy

Valeriana jatamansii
Indian Valerian, Nard

H6 *Caprifoliaceae family.* Clusters of small, sweetly
 scented, snow white flowers. Mid-green leaves,
deeply divided & toothed around the edges.
 Native of the Himalayas & Afghanistan.

herbaceous perennial
^up to 60cm «90cm»
A sun, partial shade
S chalk, clay, loam, sand
pH universal
H clump
! do not self medicate

Valeriana officinalis
Valerian

H4 *Caprifoliaceae family.* Clusters of small white
flowers that are often tinged with pink. Mid-
green leaves, deeply divided & toothed around
the edges. Cats think of the root as an elixir.

herbaceous perennial
^up to 1.2m «90cm»
A sun, partial shade
S chalk, clay, loam, sand
pH universal
H upright
! do not self medicate

Viola cornuta 'Sawyers Black'
Sawyers Black Violet

H6 *Violaceae family.* Small purple/black mini
pansy flowers. Oval or heart-shaped, toothed,
green leaves. The flowers are edible.

perennial
^36cm «36cm»
A sun, partial shade
S clay, loam, sand,
free draining
pH universal
H clump

Viola odorata
Sweet Violet

H6

Violaceae family. White or dark purple or cream sweetly scented flowers. Broad pointed heart-shaped green leaves. Flowers can be used to flavour oils & vinegars, or added to cakes & salads.

perennial
^15cm «30cm»
A sun, partial shade
S clay, loam, sand,
   free draining
pH universal
H clump

Viola riviniana
Dog Violet

H6

Violaceae family. Purple flowers with a pale spur. Heart-shaped mid-green leaves. The flowers are edible; add to sweet or savory salads.

perennial
^20cm «30cm»
A sun, partial shade
S clay, loam, sand,
   free draining
pH universal
H clump

Viola riviniana 'Rosea'
Pink Dog Violet

H6

Violaceae family. Rose-coloured flowers with a pale spur. Heart-shaped, mid-green leaves. The flowers are edible, add to sweet or savory salads.

perennial
^20cm «30cm»
A sun, partial shade
S clay, loam, sand,
   free draining
pH universal
H clump

Viola soraria 'Albiflora'
White Violet

H6 *Violaceae family.* Beautiful large white flowers. Broadly ovate mid-green leaves. The flowers are edible, great in salads, both savory & sweet.

 perennial
^20cm «40cm»
A sun, partial shade
S clay, loam, sand,
   free draining
pH universal
H clump

Viola soraria 'Freckles'
Freckles Violet

H6 *Violaceae family.* Fragrant white flowers evenly speckled with violet dots. Broadly ovate, mid green leaves. Flowers are edible, great in salads, both savory & sweet.

 perennial
^20cm «40cm»
A sun, partial shade
S clay, loam, sand,
   free draining
pH universal
H clump

Viola tricolor
Heartsease, Wild Pansy

H5 *Violaceae family.* Small tri-coloured pansy-like flowers in hues of blue, yellow, white, purple & black petals in various combinations. Oval or heart-shaped toothed, green leaves. Edible flowers.

 perennial
^36cm «36cm»
A sun, partial shade
S clay, loam, sand,
   free draining
pH universal
H clump

Vitex agnus-castus
Chaste Tree

H4 *Lamiaceae family.* Upright panicles of
fragrant lavender flowers. Aromatic mid-green
leaves. Historically the seeds were used as a
pepper substitute.

deciduous shrub
^up to 2.5m «2m»
A full sun
S chalk, loam, sand,
free draining
pH universal
H bushy
! do not self medicate

Zanthoxylum piperitum
Japanese Szechuan Pepper

H6 *Rutaceae family.* Clusters of small yellow/
green flowers, then aromatic small red fruit
surrounding black shiny seeds. Dark green
leaflets. Seed casings are used in eastern cooking.

deciduous shrub
^up to 2.5m «up to 2.5m»
A full sun
S chalk, loam, sand,
free draining
pH universal
H bushy

Zanthoxylum simulans
Chinese Szechuan Pepper

H6 *Rutaceae family.* Clusters of small yellow/
green flowers, then highly aromatic small red
fruit surrounding black shiny seeds. Mid-green
leaflets. Seed casings are used in eastern cooking.

deciduous shrub
^up to 4m «up to 4m»
A full sun
S chalk, loam, sand,
free draining
pH universal
H bushy

Herbs by Common Name

Herbs by Common Name

Herbs by Common Name

L

Herbs by Common Name

M

Herbs by Common Name

Q

R

S

Herbs by Common Name

About the Author

Jekka McVicar has worked with herbs since 1976 for which she is internationally recognised. Keen to share her knowledge and passion for herbs, Jekka has been awarded 62 RHS Gold Medals and designs herb gardens for some of the UK's best restaurants and chefs. In 2017, she was awarded the Victoria Medal of Honour in Horticulture, VMH, by the Royal Horticultural Society, and also received the Gardeners Media Guild Life Time Achievement Award in 2012.

Jekka has many published books to her name, including *Jekka's Complete Herb Book* (1994) which to date has sold over 1 million copies.

She appears frequently on national radio and writes for many national publications, as well as advising governments, chefs and members of the public on the use of herbs, most recently at her Herbetum on her Herb Farm in Bristol.

Author's Note

Herbs contain natural medicinal properties and should be treated with respect.

This book is not intended as a medicinal reference book but as a source of information. Do not take any herbal remedies if you are undergoing other courses of medicinal treatment without seeking professional advice.

Before trying herbal remedies, the reader is recommended to sample a small quantity first to establish whether there is any adverse or allergic reaction. The reader is advised not attempt self-treatment for serious or long-term problems without consulting a qualified medicinal herbalist.

Neither the Author nor the Publisher can be held responsible for any adverse reactions to the recommendations and instructions contained herein, and the use of any herb or derivative is entirely at the reader's own risk.

Acknowledgements

This book would not have been possible without
the support and encouragement from my family, Mac,
Hannah and Alistair, plus Tansy's constant, if sometimes
smelly, companionship, all depending on which dog
Chanel she has chosen to wear.

A huge thank you to everyone at Absolute for producing
a beautiful book; to my daughter for her cover; and to
my agent Martine for introducing me to Jon who shares
my love of Golden Retrievers.

And finally a humongous thank you to Jamie Oliver for
all his support over the past 18 years.

Credits

Publisher Jon Croft
Commissioning Editor Meg Boas
Senior Project Editor Emily North
Art Director Marie O'Shepherd
Junior Designer Anika Schulze
Photography Jekka McVicar
Illustration Hannah McVicar
Proofreader Margaret Haynes

BLOOMSBURY ABSOLUTE
Bloomsbury Publishing Plc
50 Bedford Square, London, WC1B 3DP, UK

BLOOMSBURY, BLOOMSBURY ABSOLUTE, the
Diana logo and the Absolute Press logo are trademarks
of Bloomsbury Publishing Plc

First published in Great Britain, 2019

A catalogue record for this book is available from the
British Library.

Library of Congress Cataloguing-in-Publication data has been
applied for.

PB: 9781472959478
ePub: 9781472959454
ePDF: 9781472959461

2 4 6 8 10 9 7 5 3 1

Printed and bound in China by C&C Offset Printing Co.

Bloomsbury Publishing Plc makes every effort to ensure
that the papers used in the manufacture of our books are
natural, recyclable products made from wood grown in well-
managed forests. Our manufacturing processes conform to
the environmental regulations of the country of origin.

To find out more about our authors and books visit
www.bloomsbury.com and sign up for our newsletters.